Canterbury's Lost Heritage

Paul Crampton

SUTTON PUBLISHING

Sutton Publishing Limited
Phoenix Mill · Thrupp · Stroud
Gloucestershire · GL5 2BU

First published 2006

British Library Cataloguing in Publication Data
A catalogue record for this book is available from the
British Library.

ISBN 0-7509-4319 X

Typeset in 10.5/13.5 Photina.
Typesetting and origination by
Sutton Publishing Limited.
Printed and bound in England by
J.H. Haynes & Co. Ltd, Sparkford.

PICTURE CREDITS

All pictures are from the author's collection unless otherwise noted.

Patrick Brown:	115 (left), 149 (top), 153 (bottom left), 164 (top)
Derek Butler:	12 (bottom), 16 (bottom), 17 (top), 58 (top), 62 (top), 64 (top), 78 (bottom), 84 (left), 87 (top), 95 (top), 156 (bottom), 162 (right), 166 (top), 172 (top left), 172 (top right)
Canterbury Archaeological Trust:	8 (top), 14 (top), 14 (bottom), 16 (top), 44 (top), 44 (bottom), 47 (top), 61 (top), 76 (top), 110 (top), 112 (top)
Canterbury Local Studies Centre:	54 (top), 55 (top), 72 (left), 114 (bottom), 122 (top), 136 (top), 136 (bottom), 137 (top), 138 (top), 152 (middle), 157 (top)
Canterbury Museums:	9 (bottom), 10 (top), 13 (bottom), 24 (bottom), 26 (bottom), 27 (top), 28 (bottom), 31 (top), 34 (top), 35 (top), 56 (top), 56 (bottom), 57 (top), 58 (bottom), 60 (top), 71 (top), 73 (top), 77 (top), 78 (top), 79 (top), 80 (top), 81 (top), 86 (bottom), 90 (top), 90 (bottom), 96 (left), 106 (bottom), 110 (top), 124 (top), 125 (top), 126 (top), 126 (bottom), 127 (top), 128 (top), 132 (left), 133 (top), 134 (top), 134 (bottom), 138 (bottom), 139 (top), 140 (top), 142 (left), 142 (right), 144 (bottom), 145 (top), 150 (top), 152 (top), 153 (top), 163 (top), 165 (top), 168 (top), 170 (top), 175 (top)
Phyllis Copping:	63 (top)
David Cousins:	158 (bottom)
Colin Dudley:	12 (top)
Bill Entwhistle:	105 (top)
Ken Gravett:	74 (top), 130 (top), 144 (top)
Ken Hando:	92 (top)
W.E. Haynes:	155 (top)
David Manners:	168 (bottom)
Ben May:	33 (left), 36 (bottom), 37 (top), 120 (bottom), 130 (bottom), 131 (top), 171 (top)
Messenger Group Newspapers:	4 (top), 38 (top), 39 (top), 45 (top), 45 (middle), 52 (top), 66 (top), 92 (middle), 99 (top), 100 (top), 101 (top), 102 (top), 106 (top), 114 (top), 116 (top), 120 (top), 121 (top), 128 (bottom), 129 (top), 135 (top), 141 (top), 149 (inset), 158 (top), 159 (top), 164 (bottom), 167 (top), 169 (top), 170 (bottom), 176 (top)
Nasons:	112 (bottom), 113 (top), 113 (middle)
Royal Commission for Historical Monuments:	15 (top), 66 (bottom), 88 (top), 88 (bottom)
Society for Promoting Christian Knowledge:	8 (bottom), 9 (top)
Alan Stingemore:	23 (top), 85 (top)
William Urry:	42 (bottom left), 89 (top), 143 (top)
Rob Williams:	84 (right), 156 (top)
Edward Wilmot:	86 (top)

CONTENTS

The Squirrel Castle. I wish that I could tell you more about this charming little folly, but I haven't been able to establish who built it or for what purpose, except for the obvious one its name implies. What I can tell you is that the Squirrel Castle stood in the backyard of blacksmith William Buddle, at 51 North Lane. The picture dates from 1955, a time when nos 50 to 54 were about to be demolished for road widening, and to accommodate an extension of North Lane car park. Note the small oast or malthouse beyond, and the weather-boarded woolstore (left), on the other side of the River Stour in Pound Lane. All the affected buildings had gone by Easter 1956, including the small oast and, sadly, the Squirrel Castle. The timber section of the old woolstore burnt down in 1977. The current picture shows the North Lane car park still very much in use, with the nearby woolstore rebuilt as flats.

INTRODUCTION

With some notable exceptions, most of the buildings featured in this book disappeared during the twentieth century. Of course, it was a century of vast changes and technological progress, but I think it is worth recalling some of the main factors and events that affected Canterbury during this period.

In 1919 the Housing and Town Planning Act established the concept of council housing, although in Canterbury nothing was done until 1925, when the City Council set up the Housing Committee under Frank Hooker. New council houses swiftly followed, mainly on semi-rural sites on the outskirts of Canterbury. At the same time, the so-called unsanitary dwellings (many of which were hundreds of years old) from which people had been moved, were finally demolished. In the mid-1930s, a second and far more substantial stretch of slum clearance was planned. No fewer than fourteen 'clearance areas' were identified, and the affected properties catalogued and photographed. The doomed houses came down in 1937 or 1938. No doubt slum clearance would have continued had it not been for the Second World War. As it happened, such schemes would not resume until 1959.

As far as the famous Blitz of Canterbury is concerned, I have already written extensively on the subject in other volumes, but it has now been widely accepted that the City Council's ruthless post-bombing clearance policy accounted for many more properties than the Luftwaffe. This was not deliberate or malicious: there was just a different attitude at the time to old buildings. The motto was 'away with the old and in with the new' and as elsewhere, the city fathers were seduced by the ideas of Corbusier and the contemporary styles exhibited at the Festival of Britain.

Meanwhile, the needs of the motor car had first been considered in the 1920s when a ring road was planned, but it wasn't until the postwar redevelopment scheme – known as the Wilson Plan – was implemented in the early 1950s that wholesale changes began. Over the next few decades, tiny lanes, established centuries before, were widened beyond recognition, and many brave buildings that had survived the attention of both friends and enemies alike succumbed to progress. In the 1960s the first two stages of the projected three-stage ring road carved wide swathes through parts of the city barely touched by the Blitz. In the event, the third stage and scheduled cross-city relief road were cancelled, despite much preparatory demolition.

Whereas postwar housing was built in more or less conventional styles, new shops and public buildings were unashamedly modernist and flat-roofed. However, great care was taken with their proportions, ensuring that they harmonised with the established 'medieval scale' of Canterbury. It wasn't until the 1960s that the sensitivity of scale was abandoned and vast developments started to appear. By this time, the tide of new building works began to encroach on areas of the city largely unaffected by the Blitz and wholesale demolition became the norm. However, it wasn't until the local government reorganisation of 1974, and the establishment of a City Council Conservation Department, that attitudes towards the city's old building stock really began to change. There was now a general recognition that tourism was Canterbury's most lucrative 'industry' – and most tourists liked to see old buildings.

From the 1990s onwards, the scales began to tip too far in the opposite direction. A concerted effort began to cleanse Canterbury of all early postwar developments, irrespective of quality or worth. With the vast majority of local people now shopping for essentials in satellite supermarkets, the city centre could be adapted for the needs of the tourist and the heritage industry. However, modernist flat-roofed shop buildings just didn't look 'olde worlde' enough for the expectant camera-clutching day tripper. Very soon, pastiche architecture – a curious mélange of older styles – became the new vernacular. Skin-thin veneers of hung tiles, fake timbering and stucco now hid the concrete frames of these rapidly emerging new buildings. The vast modern scale didn't change, though, and as a result these new 'old' buildings still sat as awkwardly against the genuinely ancient building stock of Canterbury as their modernist counterparts ever had. And with these new 'more-in-keeping' schemes came higher rents that only national chains could now afford. Sadly, many long-established local trading names disappeared as a result.

This policy came to an apocalyptic climax with the recent Whitefriars Redevelopment Scheme, where area demolition of modernist buildings became the order of the day. This recently completed shopping scheme, occupying some 11 acres of central Canterbury, is the ultimate in overblown pastiche developments – and the sad fact is this rather anonymous development could exist in any town, in any part of the country . . .

ACKNOWLEDGEMENTS

A large proportion of the photographs used in this book have come from my own collection. Nonetheless, I am grateful to the following individuals and organisations who have kindly supplied pictures: Messenger Group Newspapers, Derek Butler, Canterbury Museums, John Bowen, Canterbury Archaeological Trust, Ben May, English Heritage, Rob Williams, Canterbury Local Studies Centre, Patrick Brown, SPCK, David Manners, Nasons, Colin Dudley, Ken Hando and Phyllis Copping.

I would also like to acknowledge the following citizens and friends who are no longer with us and whose work appears in these pages: William Urry, Alan Stingemore, David Cousins, Ken Gravett and Edward Wilmot.

1
LARGER ECCLESIASTICAL FOUNDATIONS

Today, Canterbury owes its size, status and worldwide fame to two significant religious events, without which it would doubtless be just like any other English market town of Roman origin. The first of these pivotal events took place in 597, with the arrival at Canterbury of Augustine. He had come to Kent as an envoy of Pope Gregory, to introduce (reintroduce, as it turned out) Christianity to King Ethelbert, his Queen Bertha, and thence the common people. Very soon the first cathedral was established within the city walls, on the same site as the current building. Another foundation was set up outside the city walls, largely as a mausoleum, true to established Roman practice. This extramural house would later become St Augustine's Abbey.

Both religious establishments were rebuilt following the Norman Conquest: Christ Church Cathedral under the auspices of Archbishop Lanfranc, St Augustine's Abbey under Abbot Scotland. By the beginning of the twelfth century, both buildings would have been similar in appearance: two western towers, a long nave, a central crossing tower, north and south crossing transepts and a short eastern chancel. However, in little over a century, the cathedral would become by far the larger and more famous of the two foundations, owing to the second religious event. The story of Archbishop Thomas Becket has been well told in many books. Suffice to say that he was martyred in the cathedral in 1170 and, following a disastrous fire four years later, the monks seized the opportunity to rebuild the devastated east end in expanded form. The choir and chancel had already been rebuilt under Anselm in the 1130s, but now the new building would extend even further east. The wealth the cathedral acquired from the Becket pilgrimage industry enabled them to rebuild much of Lanfranc's original structure piece by piece. The nave was first, being rebuilt in the new perpendicular Gothic style between 1377 and 1405. Eventually most of Lanfranc's cathedral was replaced, except the north-west tower, which would last until 1832, and the north-west or 'Martyrdom' transept, which was considered too holy for anything other than an extensive makeover.

Following the Norman Conquest, the religious authorities had established hospitals around the outskirts of the city, variously dedicated to St John, St Jacob, St Lawrence and St Nicholas. There was also a priory dedicated to St Gregory and a nunnery known as St Sepulchre's. A second wave of religious foundations was drawn to Canterbury following the whole Becket phenomenon. These established themselves as the Blackfriars, Greyfriars and Whitefriars.

Everything except the cathedral was dissolved during the Reformation of the late 1530s. However, because various other uses were found for most of the former religious buildings, their survival into modern times was ensured. Those larger ecclesiastical houses, for which early images could be obtained, are included in the following pages.

Lanfranc's Cathedral. Lanfranc was the first archbishop to be appointed after the Norman Conquest. Unfortunately, the Saxon cathedral at Canterbury had been gutted by fire in 1067, so a complete reconstruction was considered necessary. The old structure was taken down in 1070 and rebuilding commenced from 1071. The illustration above shows how the cathedral would have looked on completion in 1077. The drawing is an alternative interpretation of what Lanfranc's original cathedral would have looked like around the time of Thomas Becket. It looks towards the great crossing tower, then known as the Angel Steeple, and features the north-west or 'Martyrdom' transept. Of course, this part of the cathedral was so named because of Becket's murder in 1170. By this time, the eastern arm of the cathedral had been extended and would be subject to an extensive rebuild after the fire of 1174. However, as much of Anselm's cathedral survives today, particularly the magnificent crypt, it will not be considered here.

The pilgrimage industry that grew up after Becket's martyrdom brought great wealth to Canterbury and its cathedral. And so, by the mid-fourteenth century, the means existed to begin rebuilding Lanfranc's section of the cathedral, which was already 300 years old. The drawing to the right shows the west end of Lanfranc's cathedral before rebuilding work began. First to be considered was the nave, which was demolished in 1377 leaving both western towers standing alone. The new lofty perpendicular nave we see today was completed in 1405. The south-west transept was then rebuilt between 1414 and 1428, and the south-west tower between 1424 and 1459. Meanwhile, the north-west tower survived until as recently as 1832. The illustration below depicts the east end of the cathedral in the early nineteenth century, with the rebuilt nave and south-west tower, and Lanfranc's original north-west tower, which by this time was well over 750 years old. Sadly, it too was to be rebuilt.

Above is Thomas Sidney Cooper's famous 1827 lithograph of the cathedral, as seen from Miller's Field. Note the asymmetrical west end, caused by the retention of Lanfranc's north-west tower. Of course, such a scene would bother few people today. In fact, the survival of a significant portion of the original Norman cathedral would be a cause for celebration. However, that was not how it was seen in the early nineteenth century, and its replacement by a facsimile of the south-west tower – so that symmetry might be restored – was considered essential. The photograph below is a 1980s view of the Martyrdom transept, as seen from the cloisters. As mentioned above, this part of Lanfranc's cathedral was never subject to a complete rebuild and still contains much eleventh-century fabric. Note the external projection of an almost complete Lanfranc spiral staircase on the far left. More eleventh-century work can be seen in the angle of the transept, with the nave to the right.

The two pictures above show surviving Lanfranc masonry from the eastern face of the south-west tower, which is preserved within the loft space of the perpendicular nave. This once external stonework had become 'buried' because the later nave was much taller than its Norman counterpart. And then, when the south-west tower itself was rebuilt, only the external faces were demolished, thus forever preserving this section. Fragments of the north-west tower survive internally, for the same reason as portions from the lower section of the original crossing tower, which had been rebuilt between 1490 and 1503.

The familiar sight of Canterbury Cathedral as we know it today. However, closer examination will reveal surviving elements dating back to the eleventh century.

St Augustine's Abbey. Unlike Archbishop Lanfranc, Abbot Scotland had an intact building to occupy when he took over after the Norman Conquest. Nonetheless, he began a rebuilding programme from 1073, starting at the east end and working westwards. The twin western towers were the last to be completed, by Abbot Hugh I (de Fleury) in about 1120. At this time the abbey and the cathedral, both Benedictine houses, would have been similar in appearance. Above is Colin Dudley's magnificent drawing of the abbey, after the construction of the Findon Gate in 1309. Below is an alternative reconstruction of the completed abbey, as it would have appeared from the mound that supported the campanile, or remote bell tower. For the rest of the medieval period, the abbey had neither the wealth nor fame of the cathedral, and so was not subject to any significant rebuilding work. Following the Reformation, the abbey was surrendered to the King in July 1538.

The Benedictine Abbey of Saints Peter and Paul and Saint Augustine Canterbury
Suggested apperance of the completed Norman Church

It was Henry VIII's intention to convert most of the abbey's domestic buildings immediately north of the church into a royal palace, and work began in the following year. The abbey itself, with the exception of the north-west tower, would not form part of this new scheme. Demolition began in 1541 and was largely complete by the end of the 1550s. The King's New Lodgings were ready in time to receive Anne of Cleves, who stayed for one night in December 1539. Hardly used by the royal family, the lodgings were subsequently leased to a succession of noble families, notably the Woottons. All this ended in 1692 when an earthquake brought down the north side of the old north-west or 'Ethelbert' tower, taking other buildings with it. This old engraving shows the romantic remains of the Ethelbert tower. Sadly, this too collapsed in October 1822. The current view was taken from Lady Wootton's Green, so named after one of the famous tenants. Although the Findon Gate still stands, little of the abbey church remains today.

St Gregory's Priory. This was a house of secular or regular canons, established by Lanfranc in the 1080s. Their role was to administer St John's Hospital, which had been established on the opposite side of Northgate at the same time. In the mid-twelfth century, the order was changed to one of Augustinian canons and the priory buildings were considerably extended. The last great building work at St Gregory's appears to have been the bell tower, which was completed by the late fifteenth century. The priory was dissolved in 1537, although by all accounts it was already in a run-down state. The church building was demolished shortly afterwards and the Prior's Lodging House leased out to a succession of learned gentlemen. These two illustrations show the surviving Prior's Lodging. The drawing above depicts the view as seen from the east and the former cloister area in 1787. The one below gives the view from the north-west in 1848, prior to final demolition. The bell tower also survived until this time, but is depicted only in the more recent of the two drawings.

By the early sixteenth century, houses had been built along the Northgate frontage, thus hiding the priory from view. This necessitated the construction of a new gatehouse for access to the priory complex, and this extended from the street line to the south end of the lodging house or the base of the tower. This late medieval gatehouse can be seen on the far right of the 1848 engraving opposite. It survived the last phase of demolition, only to be pulled down following bomb damage in 1942. To the right the range of late medieval houses on the Northgate frontage can be seen, with the site of the mostly demolished gate in the foreground. Note that the patch of exposed timberwork (centre) on the adjacent building exactly matches that on the 1848 drawing. All the ancient houses were subsequently pulled down. The current view shows the new college building, in a hideous pastiche of styles, which replaced the 1960s post office sorting building on the same site.

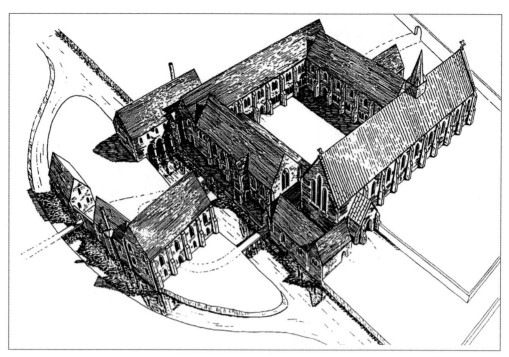

The Blackfriars. The virtual monopoly held by the Benedictine order in Canterbury ended in the early thirteenth century when a group of Dominican brothers arrived. They were granted land in the north-west quadrant of the city and began building on either side of the River Stour in 1236. Much of the subsequent work was sponsored by King Henry III, and it was largely completed by 1260. The illustration above, from the Canterbury Archaeological Trust, shows the completed friary complex from the south-west. Note the guest hall, on its own, on the west bank of the river. The Blackfriars were dissolved in 1538 but the buildings survived via conversion into a weaving factory for Walloon refugees. Even so, the church building – along the south side of the cloister – was pulled down in the seventeenth century. The engraving below, from the mid-eighteenth century, depicts the remaining Blackfriars buildings, looking east from just by the surviving guest hall.

It is unclear when the other lost Blackfriars buildings were demolished. A map of 1777 shows the range north of the original cloister still standing – as does the engraving opposite – but with the shorter eastern range gone. However, it is likely that the long north range was finally pulled down in the early nineteenth century, in advance of the residential development of the area and the creation of Blackfriars Street. This just left the remote guest hall and the former refectory block that once formed the western range of the cloister. The latter is seen in the photograph above, taken from the 'new' Blackfriars Street, following its conversion into a Unitarian chapel. Restoration to something like its original appearance was undertaken in the 1920s as an alternative to demolition. The current picture shows how successful this work was. The guest hall, on the opposite bank of the river, has also undergone similar restoration work.

The Greyfriars. The Franciscan Greyfriars followed the Dominican Blackfriars in establishing a friary in Canterbury. Having arrived in 1224, a band of five brothers was given a plot of land behind the Poor Priest's Hospital in Stour Street. Building work began in 1267, north of the River Stour, and was completed by 1325. Further land was acquired, eventually totalling some 18 acres of pasture, orchards and gardens, extending over much of the south-west quadrant of the city. The drawing above is an imaginative modern reconstruction of how Greyfriars might have looked in its prime. The large gable-ended wall to the right is the east end of the friary church. Following its dissolution in 1538, the site was sold off and the church building quickly demolished. The estate was eventually acquired by the poet Sir Richard Lovelace in 1565. By the early nineteenth century, when the drawing below was done, only the former friary refectory still stood, among post-medieval add-ons and fragments of other Greyfriars buildings.

In medieval times, one of the access points to the Greyfriars was along a passage that extended from a small gatehouse on St Peter's Street up to the north door of the church. The passage then continued through the church building, effectively dividing chancel from nave. Standing fragments of the west wall of the medieval chancel with the passageway beyond it can be seen above left. Greyfriars passage was in use until the 1980s and has been shamefully blocked ever since. The stone jambs of a late medieval doorway (above right) were reused in a wall from Richard Lovelace's tenure. Below is the surviving refectory building of the Greyfriars that straddles the river, as it did nearly 700 years ago. A suggestion made by visiting archaeologists from TV's *Time Team* that this was an early post-medieval folly, built from demolition material, was met with much resistance from the city's own historians.

Unfinished Carmelite Nunnery. Mary Hales, last of the famous Canterbury Hales family, had become a Carmelite nun at an early age. She then exhausted the family funds trying to establish a convent in the grounds of Hales Place. Having chosen a relatively flat site to the north-east of the mansion, work began in 1864 to a design by Edward Welby Pugin. Sadly the money ran out and, as can be seen in this old photograph, most of the nunnery complex never rose above the first level. Mary declared herself bankrupt in 1880 and the entire Hales Place estate was sold to exiled Jesuits, who soon established St Mary's College (see Chapters 4 and 7). The college capped off the incomplete walls and the strange structure survived until 1928, when the vast majority of the estate's buildings were demolished. The site of the lost nunnery is now crossed by Long Meadow Way and Copinger Close, as can be seen in the current view.

2
RETAIL & BUSINESS PREMISES

As far as shops and businesses are concerned, Canterbury differs little from any other town in the early twenty-first century. In fact, for the first forty years of the twentieth century Canterbury operated like a typical English market town. The main street was full of little shops, with a large proportion of the businesses being run by local people, for the local population. The late 1930s, however, brought a subtle change. By then, the main drag boasted a Woolworths, a W.H. Smith and a Marks and Spencer. What's more, groups of smaller shop buildings were giving way to large chain store 'bazaars'. And this trend would have continued had the war not intervened.

In the main Blitz of June 1942, all but one shop in St George's Street – then the most prestigious shopping thoroughfare in the city – was destroyed. The story was not so bad in parallel Burgate Street, but even here many retail premises were lost. As was the case in other affected towns and cities, surviving shops offered space for the bombed-out businesses – often direct competitors – in their own buildings. Other shop buildings, often with both upper storeys blown away, continued to trade in what was left, usually displaying the defiant 'business as usual' sign. Later, in the immediate postwar years, prefabricated 'ministry huts' were erected on flattened sites, and businesses were able to continue until the city could be redeveloped or rebuilt.

A large part of Canterbury's postwar redevelopment took place in the 1950s. Moderately sized shops were still the order of the day and many bombed-out businesses, such as MacFisheries, W.H. Smith and the Sun Assurance Company, returned to their old sites, in new premises. It was in the 1960s that large shop premises were built, employing a scale that, for the first time, began to challenge Canterbury Cathedral's centuries-long dominance of the city skyline. At the same time, more national chains claimed their places in the Canterbury retail scene. During this decade, traffic was still being encouraged to penetrate the city walls, and four massive multi-storey car parks were planned to accommodate them.

The 1970s and 1980s were the decades when further radical changes occurred, changes that would alter the way we shopped. As was the case almost everywhere else, large supermarkets began establishing themselves on the city boundaries, and at the same time, pedestrianisation began pushing cars out of the city centre. Inevitably, the smaller Canterbury businesses suffered and much-loved local names began to disappear from the main city thoroughfares.

Butchery Lane   29   27   25

Nos 24 to 29 St George's Street. The north side of St George's Street was all but wiped out in the June 1942 Blitz. Destroyed were a vast range of interesting buildings from many centuries, and displaced were an array of varied businesses. Here, we are considering nos 29 to 24, as shown above, which depicts the street as it was in about 1939. The businesses of note are, left to right, Montague Burton, tailors (no. 29), Taylor Bros, corn merchants (no. 28), Robart Crofts, chemist (no. 27), and then the elaborate neoclassical façade of the Corn Exchange and Longmarket building. Built into its frontage, shown on the right, is Hamilton, wine merchants (no. 26), followed by the National Provincial Bank (no. 25) and World's Stores, grocer (no. 24). Below is an earlier view of nos 25 and 26, dating from around 1903. Note that the frontage of no. 25 (right) is yet to receive the elaborate neoclassical treatment that it bears in the above drawing.

HILTON C. PRICE,
Wine, Spirit & Cigar Merchant,
26 St. George's Street,
CANTERBURY.

Opposite: As mentioned in Chapter 9, the Corn Exchange frontage stood intact after the bombing, but was soon demolished. The top photograph dates from the late 1940s and shows a fragment of the old frontage that was retained because it included a pillar box, and was also part of Hamilton Wine Merchants. Also note the many prefabricated shops that stood on the flattened Longmarket site from 1947 until 1959, after which they gave way to a modernist development, featured later in this chapter. The current picture is dominated by the early 1990s Longmarket scheme that attempted to reintroduce older architectural styles, but on a vastly inflated scale. The modest building on the right dates from the early to mid-1950s and has, thus far, escaped the purge.

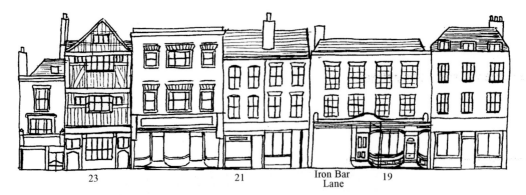

23   21   Iron Bar 19
              Lane

Nos 18 to 23 St George's Street. This section of the street contained the following shops and businesses of note, left to right: Barclays Bank (no. 23), Dolcis Shoe Co. (no. 22), Maypole Dairy (no. 21) and W.R. Cox, greengrocer (no. 20). There was then the junction into Iron Bar Lane, which took the form of a passageway beneath the upper storeys of the building at no. 19. On the other side of the lane were Wilson & Waller, tailors (no. 19), and Cyco-Rado Ltd, wireless engineers (no. 18). The photograph below is an interesting close-up study of the Barclays premises at no. 23. Despite first appearances this is not an old building, having been constructed between the wars.

Opposite: Following the June 1942 raid, when much destruction had been caused by incendiary bombs, the only building deemed salvageable in this part of St George's Street was Barclays Bank, even though it had been completely fire-gutted. And so, in the weeks that followed, the upper storeys were removed and the ground-floor bank hall returned to a state fit for business. It is seen here as such, in 1949, surrounded by the flattened sites of its less fortunate neighbours. Reconstruction in this part of St George's Street began in 1952 and had been completed by 1955. The current view shows those early 1950s buildings still very much in evidence, and in more or less the state in which they were built.

16   13-12   Canterbury Lane

Nos 9 to 17 St George's Street. This slightly longer section of the street stretched from no. 17 down to the west side of Canterbury Lane. The main businesses were, left to right, W.H. Smith (no. 17), Thomas Goodman, cutler (no. 16), Wards, confectioner (no. 15), Pettit, tobacconist (no. 14), David Greig Ltd (nos 12 and 13), Widger & Co, wallpaper merchants (no. 11), Gambell & Son, outfitters (no. 10), and Arthur Loyns, baker (no. 9). This part of St George's Street contained some impressive timber-framed buildings, as can be seen in the illustration above and in the photograph below, which features nos 15 and 16. Both are likely to have dated from the seventeenth century but had been modernised in successive centuries. It is interesting to note that, whereas no. 16 (left) has had hung tiles added to its otherwise original frontage, no. 15 (right) has been more extensively 'Georgianised' by having the upper jettied storey cut back and a new façade constructed of mathematical tiles, which cleverly imitate brickwork.

Opposite: After the main Blitz of Canterbury, little remained in this largely timber-framed section of St George's Street other than a few scorched party walls and some isolated chimney stacks. As a result, the demolition gangs quickly got to work along here, as can be seen in the top photograph from mid-June 1942. This section of the street remained a flattened, buddleia-covered wasteland until late 1951, when the first of the new shops began to emerge. Reconstruction here had been completed by 1956. The current picture shows those 1950s shop buildings in a largely unaltered state.

6   4   3   1 Burgate
                                                                                                    Lane

Nos 1 to 8 St George's Street. The last study section contains all the buildings between Canterbury Lane and Burgate Lane. Those of note were as follows: Crafts Shoe Co. (no. 8), Importers, tea merchants (no. 7), the White Lion public house (no. 6), and then Mrs E.L. Bing in the house behind the church (no. 5). Next there was St George's Church itself, which also features in Chapter 7. This was followed by François Eldonne, gowns and millinery (no. 4), the County Hall (no. 3a), and then Martin's Ltd, drapers (nos 1 to 3). The accompanying picture shows a large part of the Martin's store, standing at the corner of St George's Street with Burgate Lane. This firm had one of the highest square footages of retail space in all of Canterbury.

Only the gutted shell of St George's Church survived the 1942 Blitz. Ten years later, just the tumbledown tower remained. Redevelopment of the area finally got under way in 1954 and was largely complete by 1957. As part of the reconstruction scheme a new enclave of shops was built around the restored church tower. This development can be seen in the picture above, which dates from about 1957. The shops around the tower were taken down in 1991 and, following an extensive archaeological investigation, were replaced by the much denser scheme below.

Nos 82 to 84 St Dunstan's Street. This undoubted late medieval range was captured in the 1890s, not long before it was pulled down. Note how low the ground floor-jetty is, when compared to the buildings on either side. In fact, head clearance, as well as steps down, had to be provided in the right-hand doorway. It would also seem that about a third of the steeply pitched roof to the right had either collapsed or been removed. At the time of this picture, part of the old shop sold fresh oysters, brought from Whitstable every day. Following demolition, three substantial brick shops with living accommodation above were constructed on the site, as can be seen in the picture below. Also note that the building on the right (no. 81) has since been stripped of its later exterior to reveal the original 'Wealden'-type timber frame beneath. This came to light following a fire in 1985.

The Old Post Office (28 High Street). No. 28 was the middle property and the largest of three houses in a Regency period development, which stood between Stour Street and Eastbridge Hospital. The old picture dates from the 1880s. Originally built for the owner of Neame's soap and candle factory in Stour Street, this large house had been purchased by the post office in 1868, when the original office in St George's Street proved too small for this ever expanding service. And then in 1898, the post office authorities also purchased the soap factory behind, with a view to further expansion. Both house and factory were subsequently demolished. The subsequent 'General Post and Telegraph Office', opened in 1908. Interestingly, its familiar façade shows a hint of art nouveau style, then in fashion. This imposing building was, until recently, Methvens bookshop, and the post office has moved next door (left).

No. 11 The Parade. On the left are the premises of the London and County Bank, on the south side of The Parade, in the early 1880s. Also note the access gates to St Andrew's Church to the right (see Chapter 5), which would soon be replaced by an elaborate porch building. When the old photograph was taken, the large late seventeenth-century bank building – probably a former merchant's house – was about to be pulled down to make way for more prestigious-looking bank premises. Designed by Canterbury architect John Green Hall in a Venetian-influenced style, the replacement building went up in 1884 and 1885. It survives today, as can be seen on the right, and is now occupied by NatWest. The church lobby was pulled down in 1956 and replaced by a narrow shop that has since been absorbed by the bank.

Opposite: Nos 10 to 13 Sun Street. This early photograph probably dates from the late 1850s and features a row of late medieval three-storey shop buildings in Sun Street, just off the famous Buttermarket. Note that Christ Church Gate and the main access to the cathedral is visible on the far right. Also of interest are the many advertisements painted on the later Georgian façades of the structures in question. In 1865, a large fire, which began in the High Street behind, spread across to Sun Street and destroyed all of the featured buildings. The same fire also accounted for a good two-thirds of the famous Chequers of Hope Inn (see Chapter 5). The current picture depicts the large mock-seventeenth-century buildings that were constructed in the resultant fire gap. The restored Christ Church Gate also shows up to good effect. It is also interesting to note that today, large crowds of tourists have replaced the few local people seen 150 years before.

Nos 11 and 12 Lower Bridge Street. Not all retail buildings in Canterbury started life as shops. Such was the case for the old Co-op premises in Lower Bridge Street. The structure started life as St George's theatre and cinema in 1915. This would account for the grandeur of its façade, as can clearly be seen. In 1934, the Regal opened on the opposite corner of the St George's Crossroads and the former theatre and cinema building was consequently converted for retail use. This trans-formation required the construction of a large rear extension. Unfortunately, in the June 1942 Blitz, this newer rear portion of the Co-op building was badly damaged. However, as early postwar redevelopment plans designated the site of the Co-op for the new ring road, repairs were only rudimentary. The rear section of the Co-op complex, which backed on to Burgate Lane, can be seen in the picture below, taken from St George's Street in January 1961. Note the clear evidence of unrepaired Blitz damage.

As previously stated, the Co-op site was blighted by the ring road plans from as early as the mid-1940s. Demolition finally took place in April 1961, but only after new premises for the Co-op had been built on the west corner of St George's Street and Burgate Lane. The picture above, with the two on the page opposite, shows the old Co-op premises during its last months. The surviving part of the 1930s rear extension can clearly be seen, as can the empty scrub-covered site of shop buildings entirely lost in the bombing. Following the 1961 clearance, the site became a convenient surface car park until 1969, when it was swallowed up by the ring road, St George's Roundabout, and a new pedestrian subway. The current picture shows the subway, as well as the early 1960s building that the Co-op moved into, which is currently part of Wilkinson's.

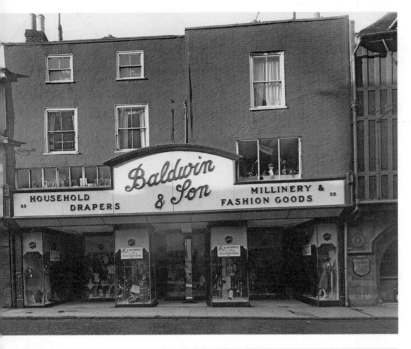

Nos 32 and 33 High Street. Many of Canterbury's ancient timber-framed buildings don't advertise their presence by showing exposed timbered façades and jetties at street elevation. Indeed, many of these old structures are hidden behind later eighteenth- or early nineteenth-century hung or mathematical tiles, in an attempt at 'Georgianisation'. Such was the case with the premises of Baldwin & Son in the High Street. The shop as it appeared in 1952 is shown above. At the time, Baldwin's was one of the city's most popular ladies' outfitters. What we see here is, of course, a Georgian frontage covering what would have been two original shop buildings. The one on the left was the wider of the two, as can be seen by the vertical stagger in the later front elevation. The picture below allows us to peep over the parapet, as it were, and see the original late fifteenth- or early sixteenth-century hipped roofs.

Opposite: The top picture shows the rear of the Baldwin premises, as seen from a parking area off White Horse Lane, summer 1969. Unlike the front, the rear of the two original buildings that made up Baldwin's did not disguise their true antiquity. Note that the wider of the two buildings (right) had a long sloping hipped end, as well as a rather interesting staircase tower. The narrower structure had a staggered roofline that terminated in a tiled gable-end at the rear. The shop was empty by mid-1969 and, despite its undoubted age, was demolished later the same year. The replacement building, as seen in the current view, provided two new shop units facing the High Street and an extension to the adjacent County Hotel, both above and to the rear.

Opposite: The Longmarket. This small area of Canterbury also features in Chapter 9, but here we are looking at the modernist development that appeared on the Longmarket site in 1961. The top picture was taken in August of that year and clearly shows how the design deliberately allowed unobstructed views of the cathedral, which had been enjoyed since the 1942 Blitz. The modernist scheme included a Continental-style roof café, as well as many small and useful shops. However, the design never won favour with those who had more conservative tastes, and few mourned when the development was pulled down in 1990. The current picture shows today's oversized pastiche development that set an unfortunate trend for subsequent schemes.

This page: No. 7 St George's Street. One of the city's finest postwar buildings was undoubtedly the National Provincial bank building on the corner of The Longmarket with St George's Street. Completed in July 1956, the external elevations incorporated such quality materials as Portland stone, slate, coloured tiles and brick. Most notable of all was the large blue clock that assisted several generations of Canterbury citizens. When demolition was announced, the author contacted English Heritage in an effort to save this superior structure. Sadly, despite a favourable response from the Postwar Steering Group, both lack of time and local council indifference defeated these efforts. The current picture shows the predictable piece of fakery that was thrown up in its place during 1996. It is for future generations to decide whether this was a worthwhile development.

No. 6 St George's Lane. Riceman's was one of the first retail developments in postwar Canterbury to be constructed on a large scale. Completed in 1962, it made no attempt to adhere to the 'medieval scale' that 1950s shops, such as those in St George's Street and Burgate, had carefully honoured. Nevertheless, Riceman's went on to become one of the most popular shops in the city. It was later dwarfed by the nearby Gravel Walk multi-storey car park in 1969, and the Whitefriars shopping scheme of the early 1970s. A comprehensive redevelopment of the Whitefriars area was begun in the late 1990s; nothing was spared within the designated zone, irrespective of use or architectural merit. Both the Riceman's building and the Riceman's name finally fell victim to this process in 2003. The current picture gives you an example of the kind of 'industrial estate-style' architecture the new scheme has adopted.

3
THE CITY GATES

Canterbury's city wall is the largest and most significant legacy of the Roman period of occupation. Constructed between 270 and 290 AD, the Roman city wall was on exactly the same line as the surviving sections we see today. Moreover, although little Roman material can be seen on the surface, much of the wall's surviving core and most of its foundations are Roman. Continuously patched up in the Roman, Saxon and Norman periods, the city wall wasn't subject to any significant rebuilding until the late fourteenth and early fifteenth centuries, when extensive reconstruction work was carried out in two stages. The city wall was breached in several places during the Civil War, and thus began its steady and inevitable decline.

The city gates have a separate and far more complicated story to tell. The original Roman circuit boasted seven gates of varying sizes and status: Worthgate, Ridingate, Burgate, Queningate, Northgate, Westgate and London Gate. Of these, the outline of the blocked Queningate can still be discerned in the city wall today, within the car park that bears its name. By the time of the Norman Conquest London Gate had disappeared, and on the other side of the city, Newingate had been established. This would later be rebuilt as St George's Gate. This period also saw churches become associated with the city gates, either establishing themselves in the chambers above a gate itself or on a space immediately adjacent. The associations are as follows: St Mary De Castro (possibly) with Worthgate, St Edmund's with Ridingate, St George's (possibly) with Newingate, St Michael's with Burgate, St Mary's with Northgate and Holy Cross with Westgate. In some cases, as the gates were rebuilt, the church was moved and established on a site nearby. The medieval period also saw a defensive gate of sorts being built across the River Stour in the St Radigund's area.

It was the widening and improvement of the main roads through the city and the coming of the stagecoach that finally did for most of the city gates, although neglect and dilapidation played their parts too. Sadly, we are left only with the Westgate today, although visible remains of Burgate, Wincheap Gate and, as previously mentioned, Queningate can still be found within the surrounding fabric. Fortunately, we have been left with some splendid representations of the city gates, many of which you will be seeing on the pages that follow.

Other gates were built within the city walls to serve the various religious foundations, all of which were walled off from the secular city. Most people are familiar with the surviving Christ Church Gate in the Buttermarket, which serves the cathedral, and the two existing extramural gates once associated with St Augustine's Abbey. There were also structural gates that protected the precincts for the Blackfriars, Whitefriars and Greyfriars, all of which have been lost. Whitefriars Gate was featured in *Yesterday's Whitefriars*, but I have included it here for the sake of completeness. Alas, I could not find any depiction of Greyfriars Gate.

Worth Gate (a Roman Work) Canterbury
6. oct 1722.

Worthgate. The Roman Worthgate survived for 1,500 years without any major rebuilding. The illustration shows a single arch some 12ft 6in wide, through which the Roman road to Lympne once passed. Archaeological evidence suggests that the gate had been constructed with guard chambers on either side, within the revetment walls that cut through the earth rampart behind. The northern chamber can be seen in the picture below, from a 1961 excavation. The building of Canterbury Castle and the resultant blocking of the road demoted Worthgate to a mere entrance to the castle courtyard. It could have been around this time that the guard chambers behind were removed. The gate was blocked up in 1548 and finally demolished in 1791, when Castle Street was pushed through the former castle grounds. Records show that the gate's ancient fabric was later reused at Lee Priory, near Littlebourne.

Wincheap Gate. This gate dates from about 1550, following the blocking of Worthgate. The first gate, which is thought to have had a building above it, was replaced in 1670 and it is this more decorative second gate that can be seen in the engraving above. A charming feature of Wincheap Gate was a pair of carved stone blocks that bade 'welcome' to those arriving in the city and 'farewell' to those leaving. The exact date of the gate's demolition is uncertain, but it is likely to be 1833: the date commemorated on the 'farewell' stone memorial set within the gate's surviving north-east brick buttress and stone plinth, as seen below, left. Today, apart from the gate's removal, the scene is little changed.

Ridingate. This was the largest and most impressive of all the Roman city gates in Canterbury. It boasted twin carriageways and large flanking turrets that contained guard chambers, as can be seen in the illustration above. It was through here that the Roman Watling Street passed on its way to Dover. Oddly, though, the corresponding London Gate at the opposite end of the city was little more than an 8ft arched postern. It is likely that the southernmost carriageway of the Ridingate fell out of use almost straight away, the gate locked and the resultant chamber used for other purposes. By the twelfth century, the southern arch had been permanently walled off to form St Edmund's Church, which also extended into the associated redundant guard chamber. The church was later extended westwards but had fallen out of use by the mid-fourteenth century and was pulled down. In the early fifteenth century, a D-shaped bastion replaced the remains of the gate's northern tower and the surviving northern arch was probably enlarged at the same time. The Ridingate existed in this state for nearly another 400 years, the drawing below showing the gate towards the end of this period.

In 1782, the ancient Ridingate was pulled down and replaced in 1799 by the brick arch shown above, as part of the improvements to the Dane John, undertaken by Alderman Simmons. This arch was then replaced by a wrought-iron bridge in 1883, which lasted until October 1970, when it was dismantled (right) and sold to Sheffield Park for further use. The current view shows today's rather uninspiring concrete Ridingate, under which Watling Street still passes. Substantial and well-recorded remains of the original Roman gate are preserved below ground.

St George's Gate. Originally referred to as 'Newingate', this structure dates from the late ninth century, when the course of the present main street was first established, and a breach used in the old Roman city wall. A proper gate probably wasn't built until the early medieval period (traces of a small passageway, flanked by narrow projecting turrets were discovered in the 1988 archaeological dig). But it wasn't until 1483 that the second more substantial St George's Gate was erected. The design was inspired by the Westgate, which was 100 years older, but St George's Gate was made from cheaper materials, namely chalk blocks faced in flint. The gate lasted until 1801, when – with 'some considerable regret' – it was dismantled to widen access to the newly constructed St George's Place. In February 1988, the drum towers' well-preserved bases were uncovered briefly and the southernmost one is shown above. Today, the outline of the old St George's Gate is marked out in the modern roadway.

Burgate. Little is known about the Roman version of Burgate, although its position over the main Roman road to Richborough would suggest an important structure. A second portal, known as St Michael's Gate, was likely to have been built in the late eleventh century, and documentary evidence would suggest it was a building that projected back into the city with the church above it. The largest and most recent gate was constructed in 1525. Materials used were brick and stone, and the edifice boasted semi-octagonal towers. By the eighteenth century, the gate structure had been roofed over and was in use as a dwelling, as depicted in Canterbury Archaeological Trust's drawing right. Burgate met its end in stages: the central gateway in 1781, the southern tower in 1809, and finally the northern tower in 1822. However, remains of the lost gate have been preserved within the structure of an adjacent cottage (see below). As with St George's Gate, the outline of Burgate can be discerned in today's carriageway.

Northgate. The elusive Roman Northgate is thought to have had a guard chamber above the road passage, and it was here, during the late Saxon period, that St Mary's Church was established. However, most illustrations show the mid-medieval rebuilding of the church consisting of a long, thin Gothic-windowed chancel with what would have been a single archway over the road beneath. The church was later extended westwards with the addition of a tower and nave. In 1791, the road arch was widened to form both an improved roadway and a pedestrian passage. The work necessitated the shoring-up of the church above with a row of wooden columns. This can be seen in the painting shown above. By 1830, this tenuous structure was finally dismantled and a new church façade erected across the surviving western section, as can be seen to the below left.

Waterlock Gate. This feature is rarely included in any assessment of the city wall's defensive gates, but I think it deserves a place here. The Waterlock Gate spanned the River Stour at St Radigund's, near the Abbott's Mill. It boasted three arches over the river, all of which were portcullis protected, which confirms its largely defensive status. The bridge, or gate, also appears to have been constructed of Caen stone, similar to the Westgate, and could well have been built at the same time. The structure was dismantled in 1769 and replaced by a ford and a spindly-looking wooden footbridge, which locals referred to as 'The Long Bridge'. A permanent brick bridge was finally put up in 1840 and it survives to this day, as the picture below makes clear.

Opposite: Blackfriars Gate. This is a fine depiction of Blackfriars Gate in a ruinous state, shortly before its demolition in 1787 for street widening: a process that was to see off most of the city's defensive gates. Blackfriars Gate dated from the early fourteenth century and stood across the junction of The Friars with St Peter's Street, as can be seen below. The elusive Greyfriars Gate stood almost opposite. Old maps show that there would also have been another, minor, Blackfriars Gate at the junction of The Friars with Best Lane and King Street, but no archaeological evidence of it has yet been found. The main buildings of the Blackfriars and Greyfriars are considered in Chapter 1.

This page: Whitefriars Gate. The top photograph from 1941 shows the gateway that once stood on the south side of St George's Street. It is doubtful that much medieval material survived in situ until modern times; this is a decorative gateway, probably put up when much of the old Augustinian friary complex was replaced by a post-medieval house. From 1881 onwards, the gate and passage beyond provided access to Simon Langton Girls' School. The structure was restored in the 1930s, under the auspices of Alderman Charles Lefevre. The undamaged gateway was demolished in June 1942, along with the Blitz-ravaged shops on either side. In the early 1950s, the new terrace of shops constructed along St George's Street's south side respected the ancient passageway, and left an opening that later gave access to the Whitefriars Shopping Centre. Sadly, in 2004, the 700-year-old footway was permanently and shamefully blocked to extend McDonald's new premises.

Longmarket Gate. This neoclassical structure provided rear access to the Corn Exchange and Longmarket complex from Burgate Street. The main façade of this imposing building could be found against St George's Street (see Chapter 9). Built in 1826, for much of its existence it also doubled as a public convenience. The Burgate-end gate survived both the Blitz and the all-too-thorough clearance operation that claimed the main building. The last traces of this little gateway disappeared in 1958, just prior to the construction of the ultra-modernist Longmarket shopping development. Below is the modern pastiche scheme that swallowed the site in the early 1990s.

4
INDIVIDUAL HOUSES

Because the medieval city was dominated by the larger ecclesiastical 'houses' and their extensive grounds, the secular sector always played second fiddle to the church as far as land occupation was concerned, and domestic properties fitted in as best they could around precinct boundaries. Of these, the terraced dwelling dominated, providing the maximum number of houses for the space available. These homes were needed for the vast workforce tied to the church and pilgrimage industry.

The larger middle-class house, with its surrounding garden, was a rare phenomenon within the centre of medieval Canterbury and only began appearing when the city expanded eastwards in the eighteenth century, starting with the creation of St George's Place, and then westwards in the Victorian era along the London and Whitstable roads.

The large houses that did exist – either within the city walls or in the immediate suburbs – came under great pressure during the early to mid-twentieth century, with the demand for land for non-domestic uses. For example, Ersham House and garden – a large Regency dwelling at the beginning of New Dover Road – was demolished between the world wars to make way for Telephone House, and an extensive garage complex, as well as the many smaller houses of Ersham Road. (Ersham House is the most elusive of places regarding any photographic record, and therefore is not included here.) Other large houses came to grief in the Blitz or in the uncompromising post-bombing demolition policy.

In the early postwar years, the acquisition of larger houses for business use continued as before, but on the whole the policy had changed to one of conversion over demolition, although the grounds were always swallowed up by car parks or other developments. Of course, these surviving former houses are not included here; instead a few more recent examples are which did, in fact, come to grief.

Some individual working-class dwellings of note have been included in this chapter, but the vast majority of such housing stock can be found in Chapter 8, where they can be seen in the proper context.

Hales Place. Probably the largest domestic house ever to have been built in the Canterbury environs, Hales Place was constructed in the 1760s on rising ground north of the city. The man responsible was Sir Edward, fifth Baronet Hales, who built his new mansion house to replace the Elizabethan Place House that once stood several hundred yards away, immediately in front of St Stephen's Church. The view above dates from the early 1880s, at a time when the last in the family line, Mary Hales, had declared herself bankrupt. Mary, who had become a Catholic nun, had exhausted the last of the family fortune trying to establish a convent in the grounds at Hales Place (see Chapter 1). The Hales Place complex (below) is shown after its expansion by exiled French Jesuits, who created the short-lived St Mary's College, a Catholic boys' school, in about 1900. Note the college chapel and its distinctive tower on the far left (see Chapter 7).

After the demise of St Mary's College, the Hales Place buildings served various functions until being put up for sale in 1925 as a going concern. Unfortunately, no buyer could be found, and over the next few years the place began to deteriorate. The 1928 sale was for the extensive grounds and dismantled building components. Above, the complex, as seen from The Drive, is shown in a stripped-out, predemolition state. Note the chapel and tower nearest the camera. Throughout the 1930s, houses began to appear on The Drive and along The Terrace, where the main buildings had stood. The once landscaped and wooded grounds were developed in the 1950s for a mixture of private and council houses. The current view (below) shows The Terrace near its junction with The Drive. A few remains can be found on what is the Hales Place housing estate today. Most notable is the charming early Victorian mortuary chapel at the bottom of Tenterden Drive. There are also a few lengths of garden wall in-between the 1950s houses, and one of the substantial brick-built gate pillars to the lost house can still be seen in a hedge at the top of The Drive.

Nos 18 and 19 Watling Street. These houses were among a handful of early seventeenth-century Jacobean-style dwellings that could once be found in Canterbury. They were probably constructed at the same time as, or were associated with, the surviving property at nos 16 and 17 (currently a solicitors' office), which had been built in about 1625 by the Mann family. The featured properties were gutted by fire in the main 'Baedeker' raid of 1 June 1942, but were retained for possible repair because of their uniqueness and charm. In the meantime, temporary office accommodation was provided within the roofless shell. The two pictures, both from 1953, were taken as a record of the structures before their demolition, and an apparent change of heart. The view above, captured from the opposite side of Watling Street, shows the creeper-clad Dutch gables to good advantage, whereas the one below features the side elevation of no. 19 and the blocked windows that had once overlooked a garden area, lost to development in the early nineteenth century.

On the right is a fascinating and probably unique view from inside one of the Dutch gables, just before demolition in 1953. Note the clinging vegetation and the scar left by the original pitched roof. Following clearance, the site would remain undeveloped for some eighteen years. During this time, it provided parking for a few vehicles, until the office scheme (below) was finally constructed.

The Holt was a large, eight-bedroom property situated just off Summer Hill in Harbledown, and only a few yards outside the official city boundary. Its rendered walls and slate roof suggest a construction period within the second quarter of the nineteenth century. It stood in 4½ acres that stretched northwards to the new Cemetery Road (later Westgate Court Avenue) and southwards towards Summer Hill, where a winding access drive led up to the house. The picture above was probably taken in 1931, the year when the property was offered for sale by auction. However, it wasn't until the early 1960s that The Holt came into Canterbury City Council ownership for conversion into an old people's welfare home. Below is the old house with its new modernist extension in 1964.

In the mid-1970s, The Holt was separated from Summer Hill by the construction of the Harbledown bypass, which also swallowed up much of the home's grounds to the south. By 1988 the property was empty and soon the entire complex was subject to demolition, as the view above dramatically demonstrates. Today, a new sheltered residential care-home complex occupies the site, as can be seen below.

Binnewith House. This impressive-looking house took its name from the 'island' on which it was built – an island created by the two branches of the River Stour. The property was built in 1810, right on the street frontage of The Friars, despite there being a large plot available behind. The older picture was taken in 1932, at a time when the Odeon Company had purchased the house from one Colonel B. Nolan. The hoarding proudly boasts the imminent construction of a new 'super cinema'. The cinema in question first opened its doors on 4 August 1933 but had to be called The Friars cinema to avoid confusion with the existing Odeon Hall in nearby St Peter's Street. When the cinema closed and was converted into the new Marlowe Theatre in the early 1980s, its splendid art deco façade was retained and incorporated into the new building, as shown below.

St Martin's Old Rectory. On 29 August 1936, the Canterbury Archaeological Society recorded this house at 14 St Martin's Hill, before its demolition for street widening. A further five terraced houses perished at the same time, some of which can just be seen behind the rectory. It was probably built in the late eighteenth or early nineteenth century, judging by its stuccoed walls and flush-fitting window frames. More terraced houses on this side of the hill were lost in the 1942 Blitz, and when the final three were pulled down in 1967, not only could further road widening take place, but also the construction of new houses set well back from the road, as shown below.

Opposite: The Priory. This seventeenth-century house stood on the northernmost corner of Lady Wootton's Green and Broad Street. As can be seen from the old photograph, much of its lower storey was constructed from reused church-type materials, no doubt recovered from the nearby ruins of St Augustine's Abbey (see Chapter 1). Such plunder was common practice in early post-medieval Canterbury. The Priory is often linked to Charles Dickens and the writing of *David Copperfield*. This, with the House of Agnes in St Dunstan's, and the two 'Uriah Heep' houses (see pages 68–9) give the city a link to the great Victorian writer. The Priory was damaged in the 1 June 1942 raid and demolished shortly afterwards. The corner site remained empty until 1955, when the Dean and Chapter built Diocesan House. That, in turn, was recently extended, using the 'cottage pastiche' style currently in favour.

This page: Sicilian Villa. Also referred to as 9 Lady Wootton's Green, this charming town house was one of a fascinating collection of dwellings that could be found on both sides of the street before the Blitz. The three little girls, proudly standing by the front door, are twins Frances and Dorothy Collard, with their little sister Phyllis in the middle. It was the last named who kindly supplied this unique picture. Just visible to the right is the rear of The Three Cups public house, the stuccoed frontage of which faced on to Broad Street. Both house and pub perished in the bombing and the all-too-thorough clearance operation that followed. In the immediate postwar period, the blitzed site was used as a car park, until the neat, unfussy row of neo-Georgian dwellings was constructed here in the late 1950s.

No. 14 The Precincts. One of the most attractive buildings in the South Precincts was this early seventeenth-century Jacobean House. The top picture was taken from The Oaks in the 1920s. The house was built under the auspices of William Master, to a four-bay Jacobean design, including the familiar Dutch-style gables. Having been considered rather small for a precincts dwelling, no. 14 was subject to several extensions over the centuries. Its last resident was Canon McNutt, who survived the destruction of his house in the main 'Baedeker' raid of 1942 (middle). The other view shows the house that stands on the site today. It was built in the 1950s, employing the austere neo-Georgian style that the Dean and Chapter favoured.

No. 12 The Precincts. By no means an old property, this Dean and Chapter house was erected in the early 1960s and saw the favoured neo-Georgian blandness incorporate some welcome stylish elements, including the copper sheet roofing. This fine house, with the adjacent South Close development, was a replacement for several older dwellings that had perished in the 1942 Blitz, one of which was dramatically torn in half by a massive bomb that created a deep crater. No. 12 and the other properties of South Close were demolished in the late 1990s to make way for a visitor reception building and education centre (below).

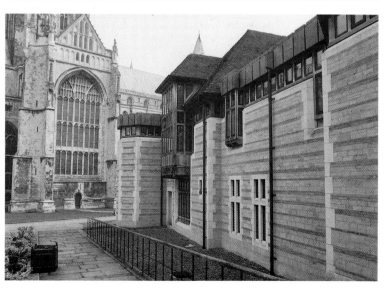

Chantry House. This late eighteenth- or early nineteenth-century house could once be found on the west side of Lower Chantry Lane. In 1941, it was photographed as part of a record (left), should the city suffer extensive damage in any subsequent bombing raids. What appears to be a brick-built structure is actually timber framing with elevations of mathematical tiling in imitation of brick. The property had an extensive walled garden that stretched down almost as far as the junction with Ivy Lane. It was named Chantry House, as early maps show this to be the site of the medieval Doges Chantry. However, the late
Dr William Urry established that the chantry was, in fact, on the opposite side of the lane. As if the 1941 picture had been tempting fate, Chantry House was indeed damaged in the bombing barely a year later. Below, the clearance gangs are finishing off what the Luftwaffe had started. Note the exposed external lathe and plaster wall, where all the mathematical tiles had been either removed or blasted off.

Above: The widening of Lower Chantry Lane in progress, *c.* 1955. Just visible, centre left, is the surviving, heavily buttressed front garden wall of Chantry House. On the far right is a complex of prefabricated, single-storey buildings, which had been put up on the lost house's former back garden, being set well back, in anticipation of the lane's planned widening. The picture clearly shows that the site of the lost Chantry House is now in the middle of today's much-widened highway. In the 1980s, the prefabs were cleared to make way for a new Safeway store. A shrub-shrouded bus stop now stands on the site of the lost house.

No. 35 North Lane – Uriah Heep's house (first candidate). What better setting could there be for the grovelling clerk's umble ome than this unassuming North Lane dwelling. No. 35, probably dating from the eighteenth century, stood directly opposite the River Stour as it circumnavigated Miller's Field, and was therefore subject to regular fogs and infrequent flooding. Next door to the right is the Woolpack Inn, of similar date and construction (see Chapter 5). Beyond these properties was a narrow common yard, and then a terrace of five houses known as Woolpack Cottages. No. 35 and its public-house neighbour were pulled down in 1905 and replaced by a row of four new properties (right). Woolpack Cottages behind finally went in the 1938 slum-clearance programme.

No. 4 Lower Chantry Lane – Uriah Heep's house (second candidate). Our other Dickensian choice is another eighteenth-century dwelling, but one situated on the opposite side of the city. No. 4 was the end property in a terrace of similar houses, although it had the distinction of having a much steeper roof-pitch than the others, and was therefore taller. So why were there two 'Uriah Heep' houses? The likely explanation is that when the North Lane property was demolished, postcard makers quickly sought out a similar house to photograph and advertise as the original umble ome. Sadly, their fun was to end in June 1942, when much of Lower Chantry Lane was devastated by bombing. No. 4 survived almost intact but as the bottom end of the terrace had been damaged, it was decided to take the whole lot down. As it happened, this prompt clearance certainly made the 1950s road widening a lot less complicated! The former Safeway superstore stands on the site today.

St George's House. This solid late Georgian house probably didn't always look so forbidding as it does in these two late 1940s photographs. By this time, the property had long since ceased to be a dwelling, and now housed several offices, including that of the Pearl Assurance Company. It was probably built in the 1790s, not long after St George's Place had been created, as part of the new national network of toll roads for stagecoach travel. Part of the house's adjacent tree-lined garden can be seen in the right hand view. The ominous notice fixed to the wall announces that the garden area had been acquired for an extension to Martin Walter's garage. Also note that the street-side elevation was not, in fact, the 'front' of the house: the more elaborate main façade was the one designed to overlook the long 'side' garden.

Above: St George's House survived for another ten years or so, sandwiched between the Regal cinema, which had snuggled up to it in 1933, and the new garage extension, which can clearly be seen on the left. Sadly, Martin Walter was hungry for even more floor space and purchased the old property for a further extension. The house finally came down to make way for it in 1958, as can be seen here. The extended garage building has now been given over to other uses, including a nightclub and a furniture store.

No. 51 Stour Street. The 1880s picture features this fine timber-framed house, which appears to date from the late sixteenth or early seventeenth centuries. It is likely that by the time this view was taken, the structure had been converted for industrial use – indeed, the 1895 street directory lists nos 47 to 52 as belonging to Williamson & Son, tanners. Note that the doorway is blocked up; the one on the right – with the cat – actually belongs to no. 50. Also of interest is the three-storey brick building to the left, at no. 52, which appears to have originated in the early Georgian period. The old houses at nos 47 to 50 were probably cleared away at the beginning of the twentieth century and replaced by the two-storey brick range that, until recently, formed part of St Mildred's Tannery. However, the current view clearly shows that no. 52 (left) survived the demolition of its immediate neighbours but was adapted from three-storey to two-storey configuration.

No. 61 Burgate Street. Taken as part of the 1941 buildings survey, this photograph captures no. 61 less than a year before its total destruction in the June 1942 'Baedeker' raid. This Georgian three-storey house was once the home of the Revd Richard Harris Barham. Better known as 'Thomas Ingoldsby', he was responsible for the anthology of short stories and poetry collectively known as 'The Ingoldsby Legends'. A plaque commemorating this fact can be seen attached to the façade. This building finished life as a solicitors' office. In the early 1950s, the blitzed site of no. 61 was used for the widening of Canterbury Lane (seen on the right in both views) and then, later in the decade, for the construction of a two-storey corner shop.

No. 7 Artillery Gardens. Such a charming little Victorian Gothic-style house would not look out of place overlooking a village green: the fact that it formed part of an early nineteenth-century development of houses for army families is all the more remarkable. In fact, no. 7 was unique; it was a one-off, and nothing like the grim terraces that surrounded it. Many of the old streets of the Northgate area and their associated terraced houses were subject to progressive slum clearance in the period from 1959 to 1968. No. 7 was included in the last area to be so considered. Sadly, such clearance schemes were all-inclusive: no flexibility whatsoever could be shown for the odd property that might enhance future street scenes by being saved. The present site of the charming little Gothic cottage, as seen in the current picture, is hardly inspiring.

5
INNS & HOTELS

I was once told that, at its peak, Canterbury had one pub for every day of the year. This turned out to be an exaggeration, as the research of the late Mr Edward Wilmot revealed. He discovered that the figure for 1692 was 115, climbing to 152 in 1862, and peaking at 165 in 1882. By the time of Edward's own pictorial survey in 1965, the figure had fallen to 75. Today, it stands at less than 50.

One of the more unusual types of hostelry, and one special to places such as Canterbury, was the pilgrim's inn. These catered for the many visitors to the Cathedral and the shrine of Thomas Becket. These places weren't provided until the turn of the fifteenth century or thereabouts, by which time the Becket cult was already on the wane. Nonetheless, vast three-storey, cellared structures were put up in the area immediately surrounding the Christ Church Gate. In Mercery Lane there were the Chequers of Hope and the Crown. On the Buttermarket were the Bullstake and the Sun. And in Burgate Street was the White Bull, among others. For pilgrims who arrived late and found the city gates barred to them, there was the White Hart in St Dunstan's, which has been known as the Falstaff since the eighteenth century. Substantial elements of these inns survive today. The Chequers was nearly lost in a fire of 1865 and is therefore featured in the following pages.

The establishment of the turnpike roads in the late eighteenth and early nineteenth centuries brought new coaching trade to the city. However, rather than build new inns, existing structures were adapted for this modern form of traffic. The Royal Fountain Hotel in St Margaret's Street, and the Coach and Horses in the High Street are good examples. Being now lost, both are featured in this chapter.

The peak in the number of pubs in the middle of the nineteenth century can partly be explained by the vast expanse in working-class housing that had spread across areas of the city, such as Northgate and St Radigund's. Many of these new streets, such as Military Road and Union Street, housed the families of soldiers stationed at the nearby barracks, and the need for a good supply of pubs is therefore understandable.

In the twentieth century, pubs were lost in the Blitz, as well as to postwar road improvements. Social changes have largely been responsible for the decline in the numbers of inns today. Home drinking is almost always as a result of a trip to the supermarket or a jolly through the Channel Tunnel, rather than a trip to the local pub's taproom with an empty jug in hand. For all these reasons, examples of lost pubs are included here.

Chequers of Hope Inn. This vast, purpose-built pilgrim's inn was constructed on a large corner plot between Mercery Lane and High Street in the mid-1390s. John Bowen's wonderful imaginative aerial illustration of the Chequers, or 'Chekers', can be seen above. When these large inns appeared in this part of the city, there had been a brief upsurge in pilgrimages following the Black Death, as vividly portrayed by Chaucer. Accommodation was provided over three floors, as well as in the extensive cellar, which could be accessed from the street. Below is the inn's central courtyard, looking south towards the High Street access point. This doorway still survives today, next to a photographic shop, but merely gives access to a small storage and service area. Only the range on the left of this illustration can be found today (see opposite).

In the post-Reformation years, most of Canterbury's pilgrim's inns, including the Chequers, were converted into separate shop units. And then, in August 1865, a fire broke out in an upholstery business that had been set up in the south-west corner of the former inn. The conflagration quickly spread throughout most of the building and attracted fire tenders from all over the city, including the military. Sadly, though, six businesses situated in some two-thirds of the former Chequers were destroyed. The early picture shows the aftermath of the fire, taken from the High Street and looking towards the cathedral. The swathe of destruction spread right over to Sun Street (see Chapter 2). Today, only the eastern range that fronts on to Mercery Lane, and a stump of the High Street's southern range, survive to remind us of how impressive the Chequers of Hope must have been in its heyday.

The Coach and Horses and the George & Dragon. The first picture is one of six lithographs created by the young Thomas Sidney Cooper in 1827. As well as other lost Canterbury buildings it features two inns on the far right that have long since disappeared. These are the Coach and Horses and the George & Dragon, the first one of which is shown with the appropriate coach outside, looking as though it is preparing for departure. Below is a rare depiction of the Coach and Horses. It appears to be a typical vernacular building of the mid-seventeenth century, but adapted to accommodate a coaching entrance that doubtless gave access to stables at the rear. This inn was demolished some time in the mid-nineteenth century – it does not appear on the 1874 Ordnance Survey map – and replaced by a shop building.

The George & Dragon survived a bit longer than its neighbour. It is seen here in the mid-1890s, closed prior to demolition. This inn, probably dating from the sixteenth century, appears as though it had originally been constructed as two separate buildings, which would explain the staggered jetty at second-floor level. Also note the mathematical tiles on the front elevation, which were added in the eighteenth century to 'Georgianise' the structure. The inn, with a smaller pub on the left known as the Greyhound, were pulled down to make way for the monolithic Beaney Institute, which opened its doors in 1898, and can be seen in the current view. James Beaney left £10,000 in his will to establish a free library and reading room for the city's working classes. A former citizen of Canterbury, the businessman had emigrated to Australia, where he underwent a rags-to-riches transformation.

This page: The Woolpack. This small public house once stood in North Lane, opposite the River Stour and Miller's Field. It adjoined a small cottage (left) that had gained a reputation as being the model for Uriah Heep's umble ome, in *David Copperfield* (see Chapter 4). The pub opened in the 1840s, to exploit the trade generated by the new Canterbury and Whitstable Railway, which once had its terminus close by. It is pictured here in 1903, just prior to its closure. The pub and famous little cottage were pulled down in 1905 and replaced by a terrace of four houses, part of which can be seen below. Behind the old inn used to be another terrace of small dwellings known as Woolpack Cottages. These were pulled down as part of the 1938 slum clearance programme.

Opposite page: The Jolly Gardener. This charmingly named pub once stood on the corner of the now-lost Cold Harbour Lane, and was addressed 3 Northgate Street. Formerly known as the Queen's Arms, the pub underwent the name change sometime in the mid-nineteenth century. The Jolly Gardener received a direct hit in the surprise daytime raid on Canterbury at the end of October 1942 and the building was flattened. A neat development of council flats appeared on the site in the late 1950s and can be seen in the current photograph. However, if redevelopment proposals for the area go ahead, then this view will soon be lost as well.

The Royal Fountain Hotel. Above is the imposing three-storey Regency-style façade of this vast hotel complex, which once stretched along much of the east side of St Margaret's Street. Claims to the establishment's 1,000-year history were obviously exaggerated, but the later frontage certainly hid elements of much older timber-framed buildings on the street frontage. Note the central carriageway passage that led through to an extensive courtyard and stabling area behind. Below is that very area, in a photograph that dates from the turn of the twentieth century. At the time, the stables were run by Mr A.W. Anderson, who also provided carriages for weddings and funerals, as well as horse-drawn buses, several of which are visible here.

The hotel was destroyed by incendiary bombs in the small hours of 1 June 1942, but the lofty façade stood up long enough for firemen to be able to use it as a firebreak, thus preventing flames from crossing St Margaret's Street. This dramatic Fisk-Moore picture was taken that same morning, after the hotel's frontage had collapsed, and all that was left for the firemen to do was damp down the smouldering remains. The site became a service car park until the 1980s, having been left vacant for so long because of the plans to build the ill-fated cross-city relief road. Today, the Marlowe Arcade shopping development graces the area, and the arcade itself echoes the lost hotel's through passage, either by accident or design.

The Rose Hotel. This was another Canterbury hotel that hid its antiquity behind a Regency façade. Left is the hotel frontage on The Parade, and part of the side elevation along the narrow Rose Lane, *c.* 1910. The view on the right was taken from Rose Lane itself in 1941, where ancient timber-framed elevations give the game away. It was said to have first opened in 1660 and may have played host to Charles II, who stayed in Canterbury on his way back to London in order to reclaim the throne. The hotel had closed by the late 1930s and a developer was negotiating to take over the site and demolish the Rose for a new shopping development. However, the outbreak of war scuppered the plans, and instead the building became the Rose Club, for servicemen.

Incendiary bombs laid waste to much of the former hotel on 1 June 1942, and the whole complex was demolished in the weeks that followed. For the next twelve years, the deeply cellared site was fenced off and the buddleia allowed free reign. The above view dates from 1953 and looks north to The Parade, at a time when amateur archaeologists had been scratching around in the city's Roman levels. Note the reused Caen stone blocks in parts of the old cellar walls, which had probably come from the ruins of St Augustine's Abbey (see Chapter 1). Today's Burton building appeared on the site in the mid-1950s.

The Nag's Head. This pub could once be found on the south side of Dover Street, near its junction with Upper Bridge Street. The first view dates from the 1920s and clearly shows the Nag's Head hugging the street frontage, and comprising several buildings. The one nearest the camera dates from the late eighteenth or early nineteenth century, whereas the middle building is likely to have originated in the seventeenth century. Note the steeper pitch to the roof in the older part of the inn. Once known as The Lilypot, this pub was a favourite of the local cattle drovers who plied their trade in the nearby cattle market, which was situated in the shadow of the city wall. Between the wars, several Canterbury pubs were rebuilt. The Nag's Head was one of them, and the second view shows the new pub nearing completion on the site of the old stable buildings. This enabled the old pub to continue trading until work had been finished.

By 1931, the old inn on the street frontage had been demolished and the new neo-Georgian Nag's Head public house and commercial hotel opened for business. The resultant space at the front then became a car park. (Part of the Holman Brothers' premises can be seen behind and to the left). The 'new' Nag's Head had a short life, being blitzed in the 1942 bombing. Trade, however, continued in a temporary prefabricated building until March 1958, when the replacement pub was opened (below). This, the fourth version of the Nag's Head, is no longer a pub in the traditional sense, and seems to have experienced an ever-changing succession of names.

The Fleur-de-Lis. The existence of this hostelry can be traced back to 1370; it was the oldest inn in the county still using its original name. Although the High Street frontage was of more recent construction (left), the main bulk of the building and the rear elevation were of medieval origin (below). The building saw continued use as an inn and hotel right up to, and including, the Second World War. In the immediate postwar years, the Fleur began to lose money, and in April 1955 was sold to local businessman Fred Riceman. Subsequently, the contents and fittings were sold off at auction and plans submitted for the building's conversion into a retail shop. These plans also included the construction of a three-storey rear extension. The City Council raised no objection, so long as the character of the Fleur was retained. Sadly, Mr Riceman was unable to raise the necessary capital and the old place was put back on the market.

The troubles for the old Fleur-de-Lis inn continued when, in February 1956, an application for the renewal of its licence was rejected. Finally, the building was sold to a firm of London developers, who announced their intention to demolish the ancient hostelry and replace it with a modern multiple store. The Canterbury Archaeological Society objected but the Mayor was by then stating that the structure was in a poor state of repair and not worth preserving! To the right is the sad sight of part of the inn's medieval rear elevation being pulled down in March 1958. Below the uninspiring replacement building. Nothing of the old building exists behind – contrary to what street-touring historians tell their audiences – although an ancient window, complete with carved medieval brackets, has been re-erected overlooking nearby White Horse Lane.

The Saracen's Head. The first photograph shows the courtyard and rear elevation of this lost pub, in the summer of 1941. The Saracen's Head was typical of a transitional form of vernacular architecture once common in Canterbury. The first two storeys are in Georgian brick, which would see almost exclusive use in the eighteenth century, whereas the top floor employs timber-framed jettied gables, common to city buildings over the preceding two centuries. Below is the pub's Burgate Street frontage, with Lower Bridge Street to the left. Alterations to the pub's front elevation, undertaken in the late nineteenth century, included new windows, stucco and the construction of the single-storey bar extension seen on the left. Unfortunately, the pub became doomed as soon as the first plans for a complete city ring road were publicly unveiled in 1945 and the widening of Lower Bridge Street was called for.

The Saracen's Head lasted for another twenty-four years, with the threat of the ring road plans constantly hanging over it. The pub finally met its end in 1969, during the building of the ring road's second stage from Wincheap Green to Broad Street: a compromise proposal that only half the pub be demolished (which was all that was necessary for the new dual carriageway) was rejected without explanation. Above is the beginning of the dismal dismantling process in the autumn of 1969. In the end, some of its ancient timbers were used in the restoration of Eastbridge Hospital on the King's Bridge. Below is the view from what was once the old pub's courtyard, and the trees stand where half the pub could still have existed had wiser opinions prevailed.

The Tower Inn. This pub, on the corner of The Causeway and Pound Lane, had closed as long ago as 1909, and for much of the mid-twentieth century served as a hairdressing salon. The building is of particular interest, consisting as it did of a corner extension from the 1840s and a converted medieval square-shaped bastion that once formed part of the city wall defences. The whole building, with its residential neighbours, was threatened with demolition for the third-stage construction of the city's ring road. The pictures show the building being prepared for demolition in about 1970 and then again in October 1975, with the early Victorian section long gone. Also in 1975, the ring road's third stage was cancelled, thus saving the old bastion. The modern view shows the recent residential extension to an old house that must be the envy of all Canterbury historians, including this one.

6

SCHOOLS

Before Forster's Educational Act of 1870, Canterbury was much like any other large town or city, as far as schools were concerned. The city had its prestigious King's School – incidentally, one of the oldest public schools in England – and a few private or Church-sponsored establishments, but for most of Canterbury's poor, education rarely went beyond what we would now call the primary school years. The act established the principle of national (secondary) schools, which would take pupils once they had advanced from the, usually, Church of England-run primary schools. A little later, and following much public demand, middle schools were established as a compromise between the fee-paying elite on one hand, and the basic state education on the other. As was the case with the Simon Langton Schools in Canterbury, established in 1881, these later became known as grammar schools.

Schools and school buildings disappear for all the same reasons as shops, churches or houses – there is no special reason why they would be treated differently. Inevitably, small private schools have always come and gone. Several of the smaller Church of England primary schools closed in July 1940, such as St George's, St Mildred's, and St Mary Bredin, and their pupils transferred to other schools, which had expanded for the purpose, such as Wincheap. Others have closed in more recent years and then amalgamated with adjacent schools. Often, the old buildings were then demolished and the site sold for other uses. Canterbury's principal senior schools are now on the outskirts of the city. The Simon Langton Boys' Schools having occupied the intramural Whitefriars site in 1959.

The early King's School. The old engraving shows the Mint Yard to the former Christ Church Priory, with the Almonry Chapel on the left and the Green Court Gate beyond. In 1540, the Old Foundation gave way to the new, and parts of the dissolved priory complex became the King's School. The former Almonry served as the main school building from 1558 until the mid-1860s. It was finally pulled down during an extensive rebuilding and refurbishment programme of the King's School, and for the next 120 years, the Mint Yard area remained expansively empty. Another rebuilding and extension programme, in the early 1980s, saw the construction of a new schoolhouse called 'Mitchinson's' on the site of the demolished Almonry, and this can be seen below. The building expansion roughly coincided with the King's School's decision to accept girls into its all-male preserve.

The Laurels. This was a self-proclaimed high-class school for girls, which stood on the south side of Watling Street. The creeper-clad frontage was photographed in the early 1900s when the school was at its height. The Laurels must have closed about the time of the First World War, for by the mid-1920s the buildings had been taken over by a land agent's business. The buildings themselves were destroyed in the June 1942 Blitz. A modernist and award-winning office development appeared on the site in 1964. The current picture clearly shows how its staggered frontage successfully resolves the change in the building line on this side of Watling Street.

The First National School. When this old house in St Dunstan's High Street was photographed during the 1930s, it was known as Railway Buildings. However, in at least one period in its long history, the place had been a small private school. Famous Canterbury artist Thomas Sidney Cooper attended this school about the time of the Napoleonic Wars. The building was destroyed in the June 1942 bombing, and for the next thirty years the site was used as a dumping ground for old cars. The National Tyre Centre premises were constructed here in the early 1970s. This building (right) now stands empty – awaiting demolition for a housing scheme.

Opposite: St Paul's Infant School. This tiny school building was situated behind the church in the appropriately named Church Street St Paul's. The school was built under the auspices of William John Chesshyre, vicar of St Paul's from 1842 until 1858. He was also responsible for the National School in nearby Broad Street, which survives to this day. St Paul's Infant School survived the Blitz, when many other buildings in this area perished. Nevertheless, it has since been closed and then demolished. The empty site is currently used as a loading area, but the scar of the long-lost school building can just be made out on the end wall of the house in the background.

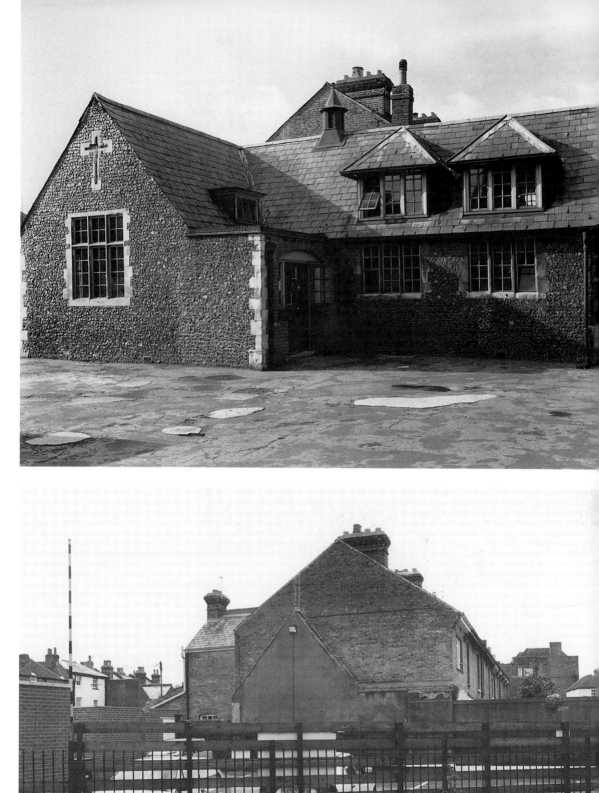

St George's Church of England Primary School. This page displays two delightful photographs by the late Mr Stanley Cousins. The one above shows St George's School from the graveyard of St George's Church, in September 1937. At the time, Mr Cousins was a teacher at this little school. The path, on the right, led from the church's north porch to the school and on to the Old Rectory garden, the evergreen trees of which are just visible on the left. A number of the ancient houses in Canterbury Lane are also visible on the far left. The photograph below was taken in July 1938, in the leafy summer shade of the tree seen above. The children of St George's School are enjoying their end-of-term concert and watching David Freeman perform 'Albert and the Lion'. The keyboard is a celeste, which was used in the church hall instead of a piano, because of lack of space.

St George's School closed in July 1940 and its pupils transferred to the Wincheap schools. The old St George's building survived the Blitz largely intact, as did the adjacent churchyard. However, as is well known, St George's Church itself was gutted and the majority of the tiny houses in Canterbury Lane were destroyed. The remains of both churchyard and school were finally cleared in 1952, prior to the redevelopment of the area. The view above shows the brick rubble from the demolished school spread out to form the foundations for a new car park, in November 1953. This view looks towards Canterbury Lane with the church tower just visible to the left, and Loyns Bakery in the centre, the only building to have survived in the lane. The current picture looks north, as does the first of the old ones, and shows today's disabled car park with the public conveniences beyond.

The Boys' Technical College. Local historian Frank Jenkins examines the medieval remains of the bell tower atop the campanile mound, in the grounds of the former St Augustine's Abbey (see Chapter 1), in January 1965. Behind are some of the buildings belonging to the Boys' Technical College, which had been converted from the former Canterbury Hospital (see Chapter 9). A new school was built in nearby Spring Lane during the late 1960s and renamed the Chaucer School. The old buildings were finally demolished in 1972. The current view, also taken from the campanile mound, shows the remains of St Augustine's Abbey with the cathedral beyond.

The Simon Langton Boys School. It dates from November 1959, shortly after the boys' school had moved to new buildings at Nackington. The brick structure, centre view, is the wing of the former girls' school, built in 1881, which survived the June 1942 Blitz. In fact, destruction was so extensive that the girls' school was forced to move elsewhere, while boys carried on in what remained at Whitefriars, supplemented by some prefabricated ministry huts, one of which is visible on the left. The old boys' school complex was levelled in the summer of 1960 and much of the area laid out as a massive car park. The Whitefriars Shopping Centre replaced the car park in the early 1970s. This, in turn, gave way to a large- scale retail development some thirty years later, and part of this can be seen below.

Holy Cross Primary School. This lost school is pictured in February 1971, at a time when its closure had been first mooted. It was opened in 1872, and became the last building in St Peter's Place before the open countryside began. And then Camden Terrace was built beyond it about ten years later (see Chapter 8). At its height, Holy Cross could accommodate some 250 children. However, by the middle of the 1960s, St Peter's Place had been joined to the new Rheims Way ring road, and the school suddenly found itself next to a busy traffic interchange, which was a far less attractive location than it had before enjoyed. The old school buildings have since been demolished and replaced by a housing development, which can be seen below.

7
CHURCHES & SMALL PLACES OF WORSHIP

In early medieval times Canterbury boasted some twenty-two parish churches, all but four of which were situated within the city walls (St Dunstan's, St Pancras, St Martin's and St Paul's being the extramural exceptions). Some of these churches were strongly associated with, and supported by, the larger ecclesiastical houses. Some of the smaller churches also started life in chambers above or alongside the established city gates (Chapter 3). The number of churches dwindled over the centuries, particularly following the Black Death in the fourteenth century. Other parishes disappeared when they were amalgamated with neighbours, only one church being subsequently enlarged or rebuilt. Consequently, such evocative names like St John The Poor (Marlowe Avenue), St Edmund's (Ridingate) and St Helen's (High Street) have vanished without trace.

The Reformation did away with many other churches, some being demolished or reused, while others were just left to rot. Historians such as Somner and Gostling record the existence of romantic-looking ruins in the post-medieval city, such as St Mary De Castro, of which only the leafy churchyard remains towards the top end of Castle Street.

In more recent times, further parish churches have been lost to amalgamation and the slow but insidious secularisation of our society. Examples are All Saints', and St Mary Bredman (both High Street). Within living memory, some redundant churches have been given over to other uses, such as Holy Cross, St Alphege, St Margaret's, and St Mary Northgate. However, there are still six functioning parish churches in and around the city today: St Peter's, St Paul's, St Martin's, St Mildred's, St Mary Bredin, and St Dunstan's.

Of the lost churches, some scraps can still be seen. The surviving towers of the blitzed St George's and demolished St Mary Magdalene are well known to most Canterbury citizens, as are the tidy ruins of St Pancras, adjacent to the equally neat remains of St Augustine's Abbey. As well as its little churchyard, there are also a few fragments of All Saints' Church remaining. Many of these lost churches can be seen on the following pages. Joining them are a few Nonconformist examples that are no longer around, and which mostly owe their origins to the more tolerant religious attitudes of the nineteenth century.

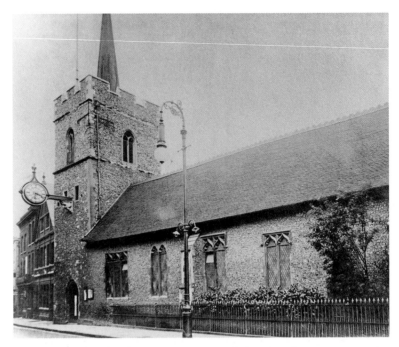

St George's Church. This is a rare view of the church as it was at the beginning of the twentieth century. Note the unfamiliar needle spire atop the otherwise familiar tower. The archaeological investigation of 1991 proved that the church originated at the end of the eleventh century, whereas the oldest surviving fabric above ground is the lower section of the tower, which dates from the twelfth century. The church may have started life a few yards to the east, as part of St George's or Newingate (see Chapter 3). The external view reflects the alterations that had taken place over the centuries, most notably with the fifteenth-century perpendicular windows along the south aisle. Below is an early twentieth-century internal photograph, from the central aisle and looks east towards the chancel. The north aisle (left) was added in 1872 using fabric from the dismantled St Mary Magdalene Church in Burgate.

The downfall of St George's Church has been well documented, not least by me. Suffice to say, however, that the building was gutted by the flames of incendiary bombs in the 'Baedeker' raid of 1 June 1942, after which it stood as a shell. Sadly, over the next ten years – as debate raged over the future of this imposing ruin – bits were progressively hacked from it. On the right the final stages of this desecration in October 1952 are shown, which saw everything but the tower demolished. Even then, the 'tumbledown' tower wasn't safe until it was restored in 1955, as part of an encircling shopping development. A larger and even more intrusive scheme replaced the original one in 1993, as can be seen below. The inset shows part of a perimeter wall that can be seen from the Littlebourne Road, just outside the city. It is entirely made of demolished stone fragments from the lost church and must have been assembled in late 1952.

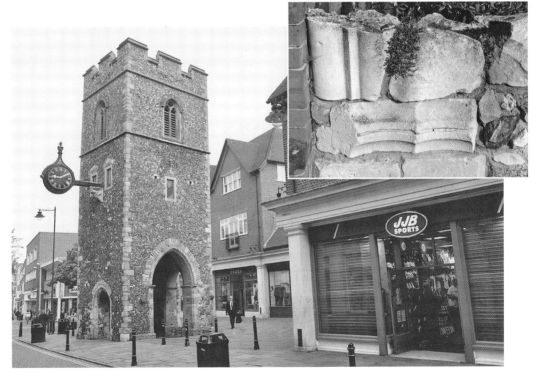

This very old photograph of St Magdalene Church probably dates from 1866 when the church was about to close. St Mary Magdalene's dated from the early thirteenth century, although the imposing tower was added in 1503. This tower is unique in Canterbury in that it is largely built from stone blocks. The parish amalgamated with that of St George's in 1681, and both buildings were kept open for worship for almost two centuries. The interior (below) probably dates from the 1880s or thereabouts. Its capitals and arcade way look familiar. This is not surprising, for when the main body of the church was dismantled in 1872, the fabric was used in the expansion and reconstruction of St George's. The cleared site in Burgate Street was used for the building of a new Roman Catholic church.

It is fortunate that when the bulk of St Mary Magdalene's Church was taken down and transported along Canterbury Lane, there was enough regard for the tower to leave it in situ as a memorial to the lost church. Above is the stone tower in the context of early twentieth-century Burgate. The scar left by the lost pitched roof of the nave is still clearly visible. Also note the railings and lamps that have long since disappeared. The 1872 destruction also left parts of the church's west wall standing, as it abutted adjacent secular buildings. These flint-built remains became exposed in the Blitz and can be seen, along with the remaining tower (above right). Featured below is another view of the wall along Littlebourne Road, which is made of stone fragments from St George's Church. However, as much of the fabric at St George's came from St Mary Magdalene's, it is safe to assume that surviving elements of the latter church also feature in this unique and historic wall.

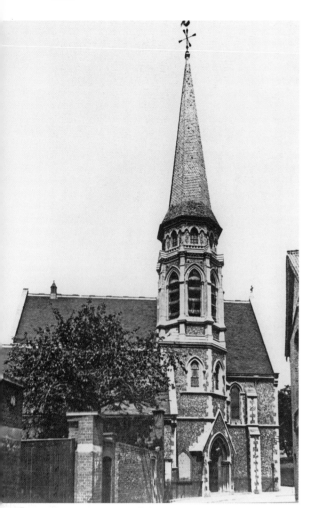 

St Mary Bredin Church. Having already been heavily featured in *Yesterday's Whitefriars*, the church is mentioned here but briefly. The archive picture features the 1860s rebuild of the original thirteenth-century building that stood on the same site. It was notable for its octagonal tower and spire, which could be seen right across the pre-war city. As with St George's, St Mary Bredin Church fell victim to incendiary bombs in June 1942, but being of relatively recent construction, there were few qualms about levelling the gutted (but intact) shell within weeks. The last fragments disappeared in 1952 to make way for the widening of Rose Lane. Subsequent road-widening projects have left much of the lost church's site covered by the modern carriageway, as the modern view shows. Only the foundations of the church's west end remain, beneath the current BHS premises.

The medieval St Andrew's Church. This little church once stood right in the middle of The Parade. It formed the eastern end of a line of buildings called Middle Row (including a water-house and conduit), which stretched from the Mercery Lane junction right up to that with Butchery Lane. The tiny single-aisled church originated in the late eleventh century and would have been quite an obstruction in the main street, with only a narrow passage on either side of it. Its parish amalgamated with that of nearby St Mary Bredman in 1681. Sadly, in 1763, this obstinate little obstacle was finally removed at the behest of the Earl of Chatham, in order to allow his troops to march through the city. A replacement church, now itself lost, was built nearby (see pages 114–15.

In 1828 All Saints' Church was rebuilt in yellow brick and set further back from the main street and Best Lane frontages. On the right is the last version of the church, with its impressive western tower. The Kings Mill next door had been replaced some twenty-six years before by Kingsbridge House, which incorporated some of the old mill remains. The church became redundant when its parish amalgamated with that of St Alphege and existed for a while as All Saints' Hall, before being demolished in 1937. A gas showroom building appeared on the site in 1953 and can be seen below in its new guise as a tea shop. In 1986, following an archaeological investigation, the outlines of the south and east walls of the original building were picked out in brick on the café courtyard. The middle picture shows a fragment of both the medieval and Regency church that can still be found in a corner of the surviving churchyard behind.

Opposite: All Saints' Church. This twelfth-century church had a very interesting history and wore many guises before it finally disappeared from the city scene. Above is an engraving from the mid-eighteenth century, which shows the church and its position near the Kingsbridge. Note the imposing south tower that clearly juts out into the main street. Sadly, this tower was removed in 1769 so that the Kingsbridge and its approaches could be widened. Below is a drawing of All Saints' as it appeared at the end of the eighteenth century. Historical accounts differ as to whether this church is a rebuild of the previous one. If you compare the two pictures it becomes clear that the south wall, with its three narrow Gothic windows, is the same. Yet the roof appears to have been rebuilt and the pitch lessened, no doubt to accommodate the new domed belfry. Note the adjacent wooden-slatted Kings Mill and the familiar Weavers on the opposite bank of the River Stour.

Above is a selected enlargement from one of Thomas Sidney Cooper's famous lithographs. Created in 1827, it features St Mary Bredman's, which had been extensively remodelled only five years before. The original building dated from the twelfth century and had been variously dubbed 'Breadman' or 'Fisherman', depending on which market happened to be nearby at the time. Its most famous associate was John Marlowe, father of the Canterbury playwright, who was churchwarden in the 1590s. At the same time as the church's remodelling, a pair of narrow three-storey shop buildings was constructed on strips of hitherto undeveloped land, one at either side. The easternmost shop was pulled down in 1885 for a redevelopment scheme. By 1897, the Blue Book was describing the church as 'not-used'. It was pulled down as redundant in 1900. However, the church's south and west walls, with the westernmost 1822 shop (left), lasted until 1959.

Top right is the south wall of St Mary Bredman's being demolished in 1959. The photograph was taken from the upper storey of one of the ancient buildings behind the church. Note that the left-hand section of this wall, including the round-topped doorway, appears to date from the original twelfth-century church, whereas the rightmost brick-built section comes from the 1822 remodelling. The demolition was to make way for a new Nason's premises (middle photograph), which would encompass the surviving buildings behind, including the Forrester's Hall. This superb development, a successful grafting of new on to old, opened in 1960. Subsequent extensions to the shop front have compromised the original design. But beware: the section of flint masonry to be found here today is a recently constructed fake.

The Georgian St Andrew's Church. When the original medieval St Andrew's was demolished in 1763, a nearby site was sought for its successor. However, it wasn't until 4 July 1774 that the red-bricked replacement church was consecrated. A site behind existing buildings, on the south side of The Parade, had eventually been purchased. The church tower is seen here peering out from the narrow gap through which access to it could be gained. The overly ornate entrance porch, complete with statue of
St Andrew, had replaced the original iron gates in the late nineteenth century. The church's vestibule, at the base of the tower, housed a few monuments that had been rescued from the earlier St Andrew's. Below is the church's east end, in a view that could be gained only from the rear of the adjacent shops, in the mid-1950s. This, the main body of the church, was invisible from the main street, being hidden by the Westminster Bank premises, which had replaced an older building in 1884.

In early 1954, the church commissioners applied to have St Andrew's demolished. It had long ceased to be a place of worship, and had latterly been referred to as St Andrew's Hall. Local protests immediately followed, owing to the church's uniqueness in Canterbury: it was the only Georgian church. In particular, the red-bricked tower was singled out for praise and suggestions were made for its preservation. Sadly, this sensible compromise was ignored and in April 1956 the entire building was taken down. The demolition photograph was taken from a building site in Rose Lane. With the church gone, the bank was able to extend its premises at the rear. At the same time, a small tobacconist shop replaced the late Victorian church porch on the Parade frontage. The shop has also since been subsumed by NatWest, as the current picture illustrates.

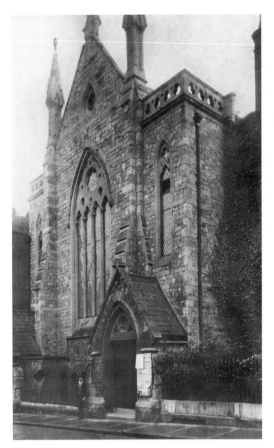

Watling Street Nonconformist Church. On the left the first version of the church, the Countess of Huntingdon's Connexion Congregational, which was built in 1863. The tall symmetrical façade of both ragstone and Bath stone stood out well in pre-war Watling Street. The church had been designed by W.F. Poulton. The interior was gutted in a minor raid of June 1942 and the surviving shell retained for possible repair. Sadly though, what was left fell victim to an explosive bomb on 31 October the same year. Either as a planned move, or an act of pragmatism, the church amalgamated with the Congregationalists of Guildhall Street in 1943 and rebuilding plans were begun. However, in the meantime, a temporary Congregational church that finally appeared in 1949 (below) was erected on the levelled Watling Street site.

The construction of a permanent Congregational Church began in June 1954, alongside the temporary building in Watling Street. Unfortunately, planning and payment problems held up the work, and so it was not until October 1958 that the new building was finally ready for worship. The new design 'a pleasing church of red brick' must surely rank among Canterbury's best postwar buildings. It is seen here in the early 1990s, by which time a further amalgamation had seen it become the United Reformed Church. When the Whitefriars Redevelopment Scheme was first mooted at the beginning of the 1990s it became clear that the 1950s church was doomed and various designs were submitted for a replacement, which would be placed on the opposite side of the road. Demolition finally took place under cover of darkness in April 2001. The site is now occupied by flats and the gaping entrance to the Whitefriars' underground service area.

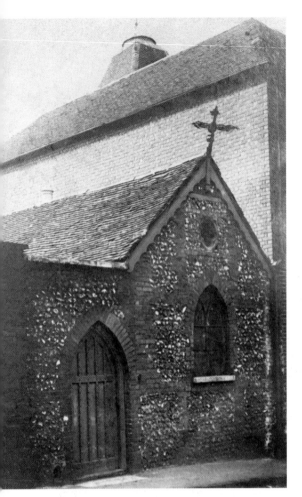 

Gas Street Chapel. This little building once stood next to the medieval castle and spent its entire existence in the forbidding shadow of the gasworks opposite. In 1875, when the Presbyterians broke away from the Congregational Church, this little chapel of brick and reused city-wall flint became their exclusive place of worship. A new Presbyterian church would soon be established at nearby Wincheap Green (see pages 120–1). In the early 1930s, when the crumbling castle keep was subject to complete refurbishment, it was also decided to rid the grounds of all encroaching developments. The chapel became a victim of this process but the later oast house next to it was spared. Today, the scar of the little lost chapel can still be discerned in the oast's east wall.

Guildhall Street Congregational Church.
This imposing Gothic-revival church
was constructed in the 'new'
thoroughfare of Guildhall Street in
1876. Designed by city architect John
Green Hall, it was one of several non-
Church of England places of worship
that appeared in Canterbury during the
third quarter of the nineteenth century.
In 1943, the church amalgamated with
that of the Countess of Huntingdon's
Connexion, whose own Watling Street
church had been lost in the Blitz a year
before. However, the Guildhall Street
property was found to be in a poor state
of repair and so joint building plans for
the Watling Street site were formulated.
A temporary church building opened
there in 1949, which finally enabled
the Guildhall Street church to be closed.
The building was subsequently
purchased by adjacent retailer William
Lefevre Ltd (currently Debenhams) who
converted it for retail use. Much of the
lower part of the Guildhall Street façade
still remains, as can be seen below.

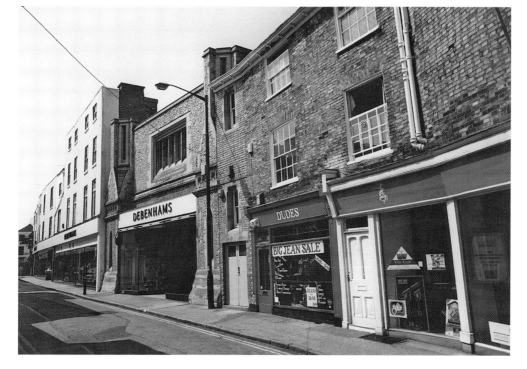

Opposite: St Andrew's Presbyterian Church. For the best part of a hundred years this church was a significant landmark on the south-west approaches to the city, and could clearly be seen from the A28 Ashford Road or the Faversham to Dover railway line. It was designed by John Green Hall and built in red brick, with Bath stone dressing, in 1880. Both pictures show the church in the context of Wincheap Green, both before and after the construction of the Wincheap Roundabout and the cutting through of the city's ring road. In the early 1970s the Presbyterians reamalgamated with the Congregationalists to become the United Reformed Church, transferring to the Congregationalists' recently constructed building in Watling Street. Afterwards, the redundant St Andrew's became a youth centre and was famous for its games of five-a-side football in the former crypt.

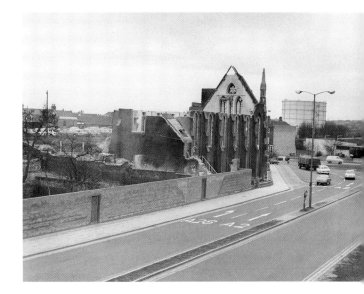

This page: Within a few years, the redundant St Andrew's Presbyterian Church was purchased by a developer and demolished in March 1973. This dramatic picture (top) was taken from the nearby pedestrian footbridge. Tragically, the planned scheme was never implemented, and for the next twenty-odd years the cleared site remained empty behind hoardings. The middle picture shows the remains of the church's crypt in 1987, after the site had been tidied up in preparation for the Queen's visit to the city (the royal party arrived by train at the nearby Canterbury East station). And then, in the early 1990s, a mixed development of offices and housing appeared on the site and that of some recently demolished late Victorian houses.

The Catholic Chapel of St Mary's College. This is a rare interior view of the chapel to the boys' seminary, which had been established at the former Hales Place mansion in the 1890s. The Hales family already owned a small private chapel associated with the house, but this had been greatly extended by the exiled French Jesuits who ran the college. (See pages 54 and 55) for an external view of the chapel, complete with the bell tower that had also been added by the Jesuits. When the Jesuits returned in the early 1920s, the empty college was put up for sale. No buyer could be found, and so the entire complex was demolished in 1928. Hales family burials were transferred from the doomed building to the former dovecot chapel off Tenterden Drive, which still exists today. Houses appeared on the site of the lost chapel and that of the former mansion in the 1930s. This one is in the Terrace.

8
STREET SCENES

The road grid we know today in central Canterbury developed from the middle to late Anglo-Saxon period. Of course, there was an earlier, well-established road grid in the Roman period, but on the whole, these first-to fourth-century streets followed an entirely different pattern and were progressively lost beneath layers of river silt and composted overgrowth, following the abandonment of the city in the fifth century after the Norman Conquest, two existing city streets were diverted to enlarge the precincts of Christchurch and St Augustine's, but generally speaking the secular city was allowed to grow around the established pattern of roads and lanes. In the thirteenth and early fourteenth centuries, the establishment of the Blackfriars, Greyfriars, and Whitefriars within the city walls would doubtless have displaced some minor lanes and a few houses, but the disruption to the street grid would not have been great. The next potential for great change to the road pattern came in the late eighteenth century with turnpikes and the ascendancy of the stagecoach, but this mostly brought about the construction of new streets, such as Guildhall Street and St George's Place, which caused comparatively little demolition. Only the old city gates and a few churches suffered as a result of these 'road improvements'.

It wasn't until the second quarter of the twentieth century that the city's street pattern and building stock changed significantly, and this can be put down to three factors: slum clearance, the Blitz and the needs of the motor car. Council houses began to appear in the 1920s and '30s, while at the same time, there were two large programmes of slum clearance. This process resumed in 1959, after the city had recovered sufficiently from the ravages of the Blitz. The postwar road plans began in earnest from the early 1960s, with the construction of a ring road in three distinct stages. During the same decade, other inner-city roads were widened or planned. Inevitably, large areas of the city that had been unaffected by the bombing gave way to the new wide roads.

Tenements in All Saints Lane. This charming watercolour was executed by E.A. Phipson in 1885 and shows a ramshackle but romantic collection of medieval cottages along the west side of this tiny lane. Of special note are the pair with the steep-pitched roofs, which can be seen in the centre. On the far right is the surviving range known as All Saints Court. Also note the gap between the two featured ranges. An 1874 map shows a building in this space but it had clearly been taken down in the intervening eleven years. The exact numbering of All Saints Lane at the time is almost impossible to work out: the street directories merely list it as containing 'small tenements'. What is known is that the two cottages disappeared at the turn of the twentieth century to be replaced by the Edwardian terrace that forms today's nos 6 to 8.

Nos 36 to 40 Stour Street. E.A. Phipson has, once again, provided us with a unique view of a group of lost buildings from late Victorian Canterbury. These, on the north side of Stour Street, are likely to have dated from the fifteenth to early nineteenth centuries. The exact date of demolition is unknown, but the 1896 Blue Book still lists individual houses, whereas its equivalent from 1910 shows only no. 36. A meat cold-storage business was subsequently established on the site, the last owners being Towers & Co. Ltd. However, it is likely that one of the old houses survived, to be brick-clad and converted for use by the cold-storage business. During the demolition of these premises in 1986, for the present housing scheme, Canterbury Archaeological Trust found the old timber frame of a fifteenth-century building. It was end-on to Stour Street and was, therefore, probably one of the structures seen above.

Staplegate Place and Cobden Place. The area between Knotts Lane, King Street, and The Borough has long been referred to as Staplegate or, earlier, Stablegate. In medieval times, the Archbishop's stables were situated here. After the Reformation, it became an area of allotments. Then, in the latter half of the eighteenth century, the first row of houses was constructed here and placed hard against the backs of those already in Knotts Lane. This was Staplegate Place (above): a terrace of some eight cheaply constructed dwellings. It wasn't until the 1840s that the rest of the site was developed in the form of two facing ranges of more substantial, brick-built three-storey houses, known as Cobden Place (below). Both views, from the mid-1930s, are taken from near the King Street entrance to the site and look towards the St Radigund's area.

All the terraced houses of Staplegate (with those in the adjacent Knotts Lane) constituted Slum Clearance Area No. 1 in the mid-1930s. Almost every affected property had been taken down by the end of 1938. The above view dates from that year and shows the cleared site with only a scatter of brick rubble here and there. It looks towards the junction of King Street and The Borough. Note the white painted building on the right: the Little Rose public house at 27 King Street, which was pulled down in 1946. The site of the lost Staplegate houses was later used for the construction of a row of lock-up garages and single-storey shops. In the last few years, these 'temporary' structures have given way to an imaginative housing development – people once more live in Staplegate.

The main raid of 1 June 1942 levelled nos 52 to 57, just when repair work – following the 1940 bombing – had been completed. The site remained empty, subject only to a few amateur archaeological investigations, until 1958 when a development of shops was started. The beginning of that reconstruction process can be seen above. The widened junction into Iron Bar Lane is in the foreground. The modernist shops on this site lasted for just over forty years and then gave way to a huge pastiche development, some units of which proved hard to let.

Opposite: Nos 52 to 57 Burgate Street. The lovely timber-framed shop buildings on the south side of Burgate Street always proved a magnet for early twentieth-century photographers. In the top picture the shops are shown in 1937 when the drabness of earlier years had been banished by liberal coats of black and white paint. Nearest the camera is the Crown Inn, and then on the opposite side of the narrow Iron Bar Lane junction, the bookshop of Carver and Staniforth at no. 56. This is followed by an antiques shop (no. 55) and the elaborate façade of the Burgate Farmhouse Tearooms. Nos 53 and 54, at the far end, comprise the Co-op grocers. On 26 October 1940 the first bombs fell within the city walls. The centre of Burgate was badly affected: some shops on the street's north side were flattened, claiming a number of casualties. The buildings in the bottom picture were badly blast damaged but survived, as can be seen.

Nos 120 to 128a Northgate. As the name suggests, Northgate was the thoroughfare that led out of the city's defensive North Gate and then headed towards Sturry. Much of the street was developed in the early nineteenth century to provide basic housing for the families of soldiers stationed at the nearby barracks, although far older buildings were still much in evidence. On the left are nos 125 to 127, which stand empty and await demolition, in April 1961. These three went ahead of the rest to make way for the construction of new premises for Bishop's Taxis & Coaches. The photograph below was taken in July 1966, by which time the adjacent houses were similarly empty and awaiting their fate. Note the minibus, standing in the recently constructed Bishop's forecourt. Nos 128 and 128a, in the foreground, date from the early twentieth century and replaced two much earlier properties on the same site.

Above are the rest of the featured properties from nos 124 to 120, as seen in July 1966. The houses seem consistent with an early nineteenth-century construction date. No. 120 (far right) had once been the premises of a knacker's yard, run by a Mr J. O'Brien. Following demolition the street was widened and then the long, red-bricked Northgate House constructed, as seen below. The taxi premises from the mid-1960s remain undisturbed.

Nos 16 to 20 Burgate Street. As already mentioned, the centre section of Burgate fared badly in the Blitz, being hit on two separate occasions. The older picture features the buildings on its north side, which would be affected. Note the fine seventeenth-century five-gabled range that constitutes nos 17 to 20 (left). The three-storey shop in the foreground is, in fact, an in-fill structure of the 1930s and it would survive the bombing, as the current picture clearly shows. Sadly, nine people were killed as a result of the sudden daylight raid in October 1940, and nos 18 to 20 flattened by the same direct hit. The resultant gap in the building line was widened by the main June 1942 night-time raid.

Opposite: Canterbury Lane. Of the five ancient little lanes that connect Burgate with the city's main thoroughfare, Canterbury Lane is one of only two today not to contain any pre-war buildings. This is a rarely seen view of the lane's west side, from around the turn of the twentieth century, taken from near its junction with St George's Street. Prominent in the foreground is the Friends' Meeting House at no. 10. Also note the typical Canterbury vernacular jettied, gabled buildings further up. Nothing on this side of the lane survived the June 1942 raid, although a bakery building and a primary school clung on along its eastern side. Both, however, were demolished in the early postwar years. Today, Canterbury Lane is much wider and best known for its taxi rank and the award-winning former David Greig building, both of which can be seen below.

Nos 50 to 67 North Lane. It is hard to believe that where North Lane car park exists today, some twenty houses and shops once stood (there was a no. 50a and 54a to account for the apparent discrepancy). And it isn't true that the Blitz was totally responsible for their destruction. These two pictures come from the 1941 building survey and show a collection of structures put up over six centuries. Seen above are nos 67 to 57, in a view taken near the junction with St Dunstan's Street. The second view (below) taken further along the lane, features nos 63 to 54. At the time of the survey, some properties were already empty, including no. 58 and Cassells former greengrocer's shop at no. 63. Of the twenty properties, exactly half were pulled down following various degrees of Blitz damage. And then in the early 1950s no. 67 (on the St Dunstan's junction) and no. 57, further down, were demolished to expand the car park that had already been established on the site.

The houses at nos 55 to 50 were to survive until February 1956, when they were pulled down in a bizarre fashion. Above are members of the civil defence within the already partly demolished shell of no. 55. They are attaching a cable to the chimney stack prior to its demolition as part of a night-time exercise. This last clearance phase stopped at no. 50. All the properties beyond were set further back and therefore did not impede the planned widening of North Lane. Today's linear car park (below) is now half a century old. A 1980s plan to extend Westgate Gardens across this tarmac-covered site sadly came to nothing.

Nos 24 to 46 Ivy Lane. These two photographs were taken in 1910 and show a lane crowded with ancient dwellings. Above is the view looking east, which features two fourteenth-century Wealden hall houses (nearest the camera), long since subdivided as nos 42 to 45 and 36 to 39 further down. Next is a ramshackle collection of seventeenth- and eighteenth-century cottages at nos 28 to 34, all of which would be lost in the Blitz. Lastly are nos 24 to 27 at the far end, standing out well with their white-rendered upper storeys. Below is a westerly looking view, prominently featuring the second Wealden hall house (nos 36 to 39). It was demolished in 1917 and replaced with the terrace at nos 35 to 40 that can be seen today. The two tiny dwellings between the two halls were originally nos 40 and 41, and are of similar medieval date. Having been extensively renovated and rebuilt in the last century, they now stand as nos 40 and 40a.

Above are the ground-floor walls of partly demolished nos 26 and 27, originally dating from the late seventeenth or early eighteenth century in 1920. Their timber-framed upper storeys had already been removed. Next door are the intact but derelict and ivy-covered pair of cottages (nos 28 and 29) that would soon be renovated, only to be flattened in the 1942 bombings. Below is the current view looking east, just like the one diagonally opposite. As can be seen, the first hall (nos 42 to 45) was much more fortunate than its neighbour and contemporary. Having been renovated in the 1920s, it came under consideration for slum clearance again in the late 1950s. Luckily, its true antiquity was recognised and noted conservationist and architect Anthony Swaine was brought in to undertake a full restoration.

Nos 2 to 4 Lady Wootton's Green and 2 to 5 The Almonry. Above are the three cottages that fronted on to Lady Wootton's Green. Of late seventeenth- or early eighteenth-century date, they stood on a site once occupied by the south end of the medieval Almonry Hall, a building associated with the nearby St Augustine's Abbey. The large chunk of medieval fabric (far right) may have been associated with the hall, and further fabric may have been incorporated into the cottages themselves. The view on the left looks northwards along The Almonry Passage, which could be accessed just to the left of the Lady Wootton's Green cottages. No. 2 The Almonry (far left), clearly incorporates the surviving north wall of the medieval hall, the original inner face of which is visible here. Nos 3 to 5 The Almonry, dating from the eighteenth century, are nearer the camera on the right.

Above is that surviving stretch of medieval wall that extended eastwards to become the north wall of 3 The Almonry. Note the stone-jamb Gothic window on the left, which must have once been a feature of the Almonry Hall. The brick-built east wall of no. 2 can be seen to the right. All of the cottages in The Almonry constituted Slum Clearance Area No. 10, but were not demolished with the other similarly designated dwellings. This could be in recognition of the fact that they incorporated medieval material. Sadly, though, all of them were badly blasted in the June 1942 Blitz, only to be demolished in the months that followed. The medieval wall stood alone for another couple of years before it too was pulled down to make way for the extension to Monastery Street. Today, a modern house called The Almonry stands on the much-reduced site.

Nos 1 to 8 Camden Terrace. This row of houses was built at the top end of St Peter's Place in the 1880s and stood immediately south of the Holy Cross School. The other properties in the street were, on average, fifty years older, and yet it was these more modern properties that were doomed. Camden Terrace can be seen standing empty in the old picture from 1961, prior to demolition. They were to make way for the St Peter's Roundabout, which would become part of the Rheims Way ring-road circuit. The current view shows today's busy traffic interchange, which will become even more choked following the forthcoming Tannery development.

Wincheap Grove. Above: this view from April 1961 shows not only further properties that were pulled down to make way for the ring road, but also an entire street that was lost because of it. To the right is the perimeter wall of the BRS depot and the junction for St Andrew's Close. To the left are the mainly nineteenth-century terraced houses that were already being stripped out prior to demolition. Over the following two years, the narrow, sloping Wincheap Grove gave way to an embankment dual carriageway that would form part of the first stage of the city's ring road, called the Rheims Way. The buildings at the top of the lane would later make way for the Wincheap Roundabout. Today, the scene is utterly changed. The only common factor is the perimeter wall to the depot, which, much curtailed, now surrounds the Habitat store.

Nos 19 to 26 Knotts Lane. Both mid-1930s pictures on this page feature the seventeenth- and eighteenth-century houses along the west side of Knotts Lane. They convey an almost romantic scene far removed from the 'no-go' area or 'red-light' district that some contemporary citizens claim it to have been. The view on the left is dominated by the impressive mid-seventeenth-century, double-jettied, three-storey house at no. 22, which was the residence of one Mrs Giles. To the right are two eighteenth-century cottages (nos 23 and 24), followed by the entrance to Knotts Passage and Knotts Square, both of which contained tiny tenements. Beyond the passage is a pair of semi-detached eighteenth-century houses at nos 25 and 26. The photograph on the right looks in the opposite direction and features nos 24 down to 19, with the surviving nineteenth-century warehouse at the far end and cottages in King Street also visible.

Opposite: Taken from the junction with King Street, the top view shows 19 to 26 Knotts Lane under demolition on 25 April 1938. Note the exposed second-storey side window of no. 22, which proves it must have stood alone for at least a short period. Demolition also revealed that the brick façades of the two-storey houses could have been late eighteenth- or early nineteenth-century replacements for their original timbered and jettied frontages. For many years, the area was a scrapyard, and then the neo-Georgian houses of the new Abbotts Place development were built here in the early 1970s, as can be seen in the current view.

A 1962 picture of houses in Stour Street, at a time when slum clearance was being considered. Nearest the camera are nos 58 and 59, which are typical of the early nineteenth-century properties that extended to no. 53 at the Rosemary Lane junction. Following demolition of the affected houses, the ground-floor walls of no. 62a were retained and for the next forty-odd years acted as a perimeter wall to a small garden area (middle). Sadly, this last fragment was recently flattened to make way for the new residential scheme below.

Opposite: Nos 53 to 62a Stour Street. The top view, from September 1960, is dominated by the early nineteenth-century brick-built 'in-fill' house at no. 62a. Next to it (far right) is a terrace of three three-storey houses (nos 60 to 62) that date from the mid-seventeenth century. Below are the charming rear elevations of the last three mentioned houses, in a view taken on 18 May 1962. By this time, all of the featured houses had been condemned as 'unfit for human habitation' in the Canterbury Compulsory Purchase order of 1961. The Canterbury Society was aggrieved by the threatened loss of nos 60 to 62. As a result the City Council announced its willingness to permit the Society to take over the properties – provided it could fund their complete renovation. Sadly, such an offer proved impossible to accept and all the affected properties were subsequently demolished.

St George's Terrace. This lost Georgian thoroughfare has already been featured in my previous books, especially *Yesterday's Whitefriars*, but a study of Canterbury's lost heritage wouldn't be complete without it. This picture, from 1932, shows the rarely seen south end of the terrace, comprising early nineteenth-century two- and three-storey town houses. On the far left, and set back in its own garden, is the detached Terrace House, which was separated from the other houses by the sloping junction for Gravel Walk that once joined St George's Terrace at this point. All the featured houses were gutted in the June 1942 Blitz and their burnt-out shells cleared away in the months that followed. Today, St George's Terrace has no houses of its own and has reverted to being the rampart walk it was in antiquity.

9
PUBLIC BUILDINGS

I n the past – even the recent past – Canterbury has always cared for its religious buildings far more than it has for those from the secular side of the coin. This is hardly surprising given the wealth of surviving medieval ecclesiastical buildings in and around the city, both intact and in ruins. In fact, one could go so far as to say that the city is so rich in upstanding church history that it can afford to destroy the substantial underground remains of such large religious houses as the Whitefriars and St Gregory's Priory in redeveloping their sites. And whereas ancient public buildings can be found in other towns and cities – such as town halls, guildhalls, corn exchanges, assembly rooms, theatres and philosophical institutions – they do not survive in Canterbury, largely for the same reason. True, the Guildhall is currently housed in a wonderful medieval church (Holy Cross), but its ancient purpose-built predecessor was pulled down some years before. The pages that follow will show that the city did indeed boast many of these old public buildings, but it also has to be acknowledged that none of them were so old as the Guildhall, which rightly starts this section.

The Guildhall. Although its external appearance did not suggest as much, this building contained elements dating back at least to the twelfth century. The first picture dates from 1897 and shows the exterior of the Guildhall, decorated for Queen Victoria's diamond jubilee. The external elevations seen here date from an extensive rebuilding programme undertaken in 1835. Note the elaborate Regency style of the High Street frontage, compared to the plainer Guildhall Street elevation. The latter named street had been first cut through in 1805. On the left is a view of the main council chamber which includes some of the medieval roofing timbers, all of which had survived the 1835 rebuild. Beyond the partition wall on the left is the Mayor's Chamber, which had its own access from Guildhall Street (just visible above).

Concerns over the condition of the ancient roof timbers, as well as the state of the supporting walls, which were found to be only a few inches thick in places, led to the progressive dismantling of the structure from 1949. Initially this had been for the purposes of repair but it eventually became permanent. The top view shows that by April 1953 only the Mayor's Chamber remained intact. This too was pulled down in 1955, prior to redevelopment of the valuable corner site for a new shop. In the clearance process an ancient pillar was discovered (inset), which once would have supported an undercroft. This twelfth-century fragment was preserved in situ and the shop built around it. The current view shows the shoe shop that has closed since the picture was taken. The staff were always happy to show visitors the old pillar in their cellar, which they'd nicknamed 'Norman'.

The Corn Exchange and Longmarket. This building and its site features more than once in this book, not least in the 'Retail Premises' section (Chapter 2). This is not surprising, for in the last 100 years the area has boasted an impressive Corn Exchange building, a bomb-site punctuated by prefabricated shops, a modernist cityscape and an oversized pastiche scheme. Here, however, we will consider the first of these. To the left is the 1824 St George's Street frontage of the building in the early years of the war, complete with war savings clock. The Longmarket was the open area below, where stalls could be set up, whereas the Corn Exchange was held in the rooms above. There was also a connecting passage that led to a small gateway in Burgate (see Chapter 3). The view below was taken around dawn on 1 June 1942, and shows firemen damping down on either side of the gutted Corn Exchange. Despite the devastating fire, the building's impressive frontage and the Burgate gateway remained largely intact.

Despite its reasonably intact state, the imposing Corn Exchange façade was pulled down in mid-June 1942. The picture above shows this process already complete, with the demolition crane removing the upper-floor supports. The haste to rid the city of the structure may have been influenced by the fact that a plan to construct a grand 'Civic Way', linking the cathedral with new council offices, had already been proposed in the immediate pre-war years. But in the meantime the site was given over to temporary prefab shops, which lasted from 1947 until 1959. The modernist shopping development survived from 1960 to 1990 (see Chapter 2) and then, following an extensive archaeological investigation, the scheme seen below was built.

The Theatre Royal. This building once occupied a large site on the eastern side of Guildhall Street. It was designed by famous cattle painter Thomas Sidney Cooper, who also bore the majority of the construction costs. He laid the foundation stone in 1860 and work was completed by the end of the following year. As can be seen, the main theatre frontage was built in a neoclassical-cum-Regency style, which would have been old-fashioned by that time. However, this style could have been chosen in order to harmonise with the adjacent Philosophical and Literary Institution (far left) or nearby Guildhall (on the opposite side of the street), both of which are featured in this chapter. The Theatre Royal was not a financial success and had to be heavily subsidised by its famous patron. It finally closed in January 1926 and had been demolished by May the following year. The middle picture shows the site being prepared for the construction of a new shop for Lefevre's, which opened in 1927 and can be seen in the bottom view.

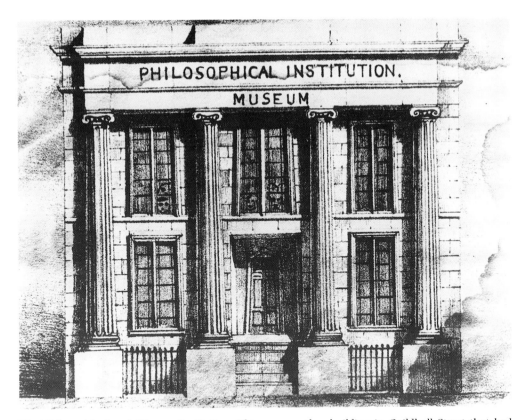

The Philosophical and Literary Institution. This was another building in Guildhall Street that had associations with Thomas Sidney Cooper. Opening in 1825, this Regency-style structure contained an exhibition or lecture space, a library and a committee room. Cooper was one of its first members. The building was finally replaced by the Beaney Institute at the end of the nineteenth century (see Chapter 5), after which it became municipal offices before being absorbed by Lefevre's (see opposite page). At one stage in its transition from institute to shop, the building was stripped of its decorative frontage (below right). The photograph below left shows the rear of the old building from Sun Yard, taken in April 1953. This rear elevation has since been eliminated by a modern shop extension.

Kent and Canterbury Hospital. The familiar theme of neoclassical architecture is continued in the design of the city's first publicly subscribed hospital. It was situated on the north side of Longport, within the walled precincts of St Augustine's Abbey (see Chapter 1) and on land that was once the lay cemetery. The central section of the hospital building was the original part, opening in 1793. The east wing was added in 1817 and the balancing west wing in 1838. Below is a view of the main hospital building at its largest, showing its proximity to the ruins of the abbey. In 1937 a new hospital complex was built in south Canterbury and almost straight away plans were laid for the former building's demolition, in order to 'reunite' the lay cemetery with the rest of the abbey remains. In the meantime, other uses were found for the old place and in the Second World War it became an emergency shelter for Blitz victims.

After the war, the former hospital transformed itself into the Boys' Technical College (see Chapter 6), which meant that my father had the dubious distinction of having his tonsils out and then going to secondary school in the same building! In the 1960s, the boys' tech moved to a fresh site and new buildings along Spring Lane, now known as The Chaucer. The old buildings lingered on until 1972 when they were finally demolished, some thirty-five years after their destruction had first been mooted. This process can be seen in the above picture, with part of the east wing already gone. In recent years, a new visitor reception centre for the abbey ruins has been built on part of the site, the bold wall-like frontage of which can be seen below.

Whitehall Public Swimming Bath. The old picture, *c.* 1937, shows an interschool swimming event involving Simon Langton Boys' and another east Kent school, possibly Harvey Grammar. It was taken from the earth bank that ran around the perimeter of this outdoor pool and looks towards the curved shallow end. The divers are, of course, using the deep end, which was nearest the Westgate Gardens. This more northerly end can better be seen in the view below. Note the poplars along the adjacent River Stour, some of which still survive. The pool was opened in 1876, measuring 375ft by 75ft, and was about 10ft deep at the Westgate end, easing to about 6ft at the halfway point. The facilities included partially open-sided changing pavilions and a large mangle to dry your costume.

The Whitehall bath was filled from a channel, which let river water in at the pool's shallow end through a sluice-gate. Consequently, the water was cold and there was always at least a foot of mud at the bottom. Sometimes more water was let in than desired, for when the adjacent River Stour was in flood the pool was likewise inundated. The above view, from 1909, shows the pool unusable owing to seasonal flooding – not that one would want a cold dip at that time of year! Swimming continued throughout the Second World War, but the pool closed for good by the beginning of the 1950s. And then, while the City Council formulated plans for a new indoor pool, the old bath was converted into a paddling pool and quickly became known as Toddlers' Cove. The new baths finally opened at Kingsmead in 1970. Today, the paddling pool has been filled in, but the curved bank of its shallow end can still be made out round the area's small car park, as shown below.

Left: The lobby building of the old Marlowe Theatre that fronted on to St Margaret's Street, November 1960. Although it appeared to date from the sixteenth century, this building was constructed in 1927. It had started life as the Central Picture Theatre, and was converted from cinema to theatre in 1951. This conversion necessitated the building of a large extension at the rear, or stage end, and this can be seen in the bottom photograph which was taken from the adjacent Rose Lane car park. The work cost £38,000 and took seven months to complete. Over the years, the old Marlowe Theatre supported many acts, both drama and music, including the annual pantomime. In March 1969, Pink Floyd even played here!

The old Marlowe Theatre was first threatened with demolition to make way for an east–west cross-city relief road. This destructive road plan seems to have been dropped by the early 1970s. Nevertheless, the theatre building was finally demolished in 1982, in order to make way for the Marlowe Arcade shopping scheme. The demolition has been dramatically captured above, which looks towards the rear 1951 extension from St Margaret's Street. Oddly enough, the new Marlowe Theatre (opposite below) was another converted cinema: the Odeon in The Friars (see Chapter 4). Today, a 1980s shop stands where the old lobby building used to be. It is currently empty and awaiting new occupants.

The Old Canterbury Baths. This ancient timber-framed building once stood in Upper Bridge Street but was purchased by builder and amateur historian Walter Cozens, and then moved to its new site on the corner of Station Road West in 1906. Cozens rebuilt the two ends of the old frame side by side, and then built a new back for it. Once open, this 'new' building contained public baths on the ground floor – an alternative to the tin bath at home – and above, Walter created a small museum. This housed all the relics and artefacts he'd uncovered over his years as a builder in the city. Sadly, this relocated building was destroyed in the June 1942 Blitz. Ironically, its former site in Upper Bridge Street remained unaffected by the bombing. New shops appeared on the site in the mid-1950s, as seen on the right.

10
INDUSTRY

Canterbury is not well known as a centre for industry and never has been. However, the city does have one major asset on which several industries did grow up, and that was the River Stour. The two main branches of this river once provided power for a series of watermills – three large ones in particular. Sadly, these are now all gone, the last one succumbing to a disastrous fire only a few years ago. The other industry that took advantage of Canterbury's many bisecting water channels was that which produced leather. Not only did the city once boast a large and extensive tanning business, but also supported several associated fellmonger businesses. Fellmongers took the hides from the abattoir and prepared them for the tanner. They also processed woollen fleeces. It is hard to believe that such a smelly business once existed right next to the Westgate Towers, where the scented flowers of the Westgate gardens can now be enjoyed. As for the tannery, it finally closed in recent years, although many of its historical buildings are currently being converted for residential use – hence its exclusion from this chapter.

As with the majority of other towns and cities, Canterbury was once responsible for its own utilities. A gasworks, electricity works, and water pumping station could once be found in and around the city, although since the establishment of national grid systemsthese are a thing of the past. Brewing was another industry that most major towns supported, not least for their own consumption. Canterbury once had three major breweries and a number of oasts and malthouses to support them. Nowadays, such activities are usually concentrated in large complexes that can produce the vast quantities needed for the modern market, such as Shepherd Neame in nearby Faversham.

Today, Canterbury leans heavily on its greatest asset for wealth creation: in other words the city's large stock of famous historical buildings – and the heritage business does not mix well with more traditional types of industry.

Abbott's Mill. This was the largest and most imposing of Canterbury's three major watermills. The six-storey, largely timber-framed structure was designed by John Smeaton, of Edison Lighthouse fame, and completed in 1792. It was the latest in a series of watermills that had existed on this site since Saxon times. The first picture dates from the 1880s and looks north from the sluice-gates upstream from the mill. At this time, the vast building was owned by Thomas Sidney Cooper, who also had possession of the nearby Westgate Mill. The second view is from the 1920s and shows the mill from the more familiar vantage point of St Radigund's Street. By this time, the mill had passed into the ownership of local firm T. Denne & Sons Ltd. Note the Miller's Arms pub on the corner of the appropriately named Mill Lane.

Opposite: On 17 October 1933 a fire broke out in Abbott's Mill. The blaze rapidly took hold of the entire structure and took several days to quench, by which time there was little left to save. The dramatic aerial view (above) shows that spectacular and memorable blaze in its latter stages. Note the large crowds that have come to witness the event. The people-lined bridge, just to the left of the fire, is the St Radigund's Bridge, which replaced the medieval Water Gate (see Chapter 3). Today the mill site is part of the riverside walk complex and is also used as a beer garden for the nearby Miller's Arms (right). The current picture also shows the few remaining pieces of mill machinery and the two mill-races, both of which serve to remind today's pub patron of what once existed there.

Westgate Mill. Variously known as Dean's, Westgate, and Hooker's Mill, this impressive building once spanned the river near the junction of North Lane with The Causeway. As was the case with nearby Abbott's Mill, there had been a mill on this site since Saxon times, although the last building dated from the late eighteenth or early nineteenth century. The impressive mill is reflected in the calm waters of the Stour in the above photograph, taken in the late 1940s. Note that the central wooden section, which spans the river and therefore contains the mill-wheels, is sandwiched between two brick-built sections that housed other parts of the milling process. The Westgate Mill again aped its loftier neighbour when, on the night of Tuesday 9 June 1954, the structure caught fire. The view below shows some of the many fire crews summoned to tackle the blaze.

The fire of 1954 destroyed Westgate Mill's central wooden section and severely damaged the taller southernmost brick section. The mill never operated again and for the following four years it stood forlorn, empty and largely open to the elements. Finally, in July 1958, the undamaged northern section was demolished to make way for improvements to the adjacent road junction. This process was undertaken by hand, so the bricks could be reused elsewhere, as can be seen above. The rest of the fire-damaged structure disappeared in gradual stages over successive years, although remains of it were still visible up to the 1990s. Below, the mill is shown – or at least a decent facsimile of it – recently rebuilt as an impressive sheltered-housing complex. Today, the foaming mill-races still exist beneath the central timber façaded section of the building, as they did in years gone by.

Barton Mill. The existence of this watermill dates back to the eleventh century and the time of Archbishop Lanfranc. For much of the medieval period it was in the hands of Christchurch Priory and essential to its brewing activities. Medieval elements still survive in the buildings associated with Barton Mill, although the last version of the mill proper dated from the late eighteenth century. The top view dates from the early twentieth century and features the largely timber-framed mill structure spanning the River Stour to the east of the city. By the late eighteenth century the mill had been given over to the making of paper. In 1951, a fire partly destroyed the loftier section of the mill, as can be seen below. It shows the affected part being dismantled before rebuilding. Luckily, at the time the main part of the mill (left) survived almost intact. Note the much older flint and stone building on the far right.

Following the 1951 fire, the affected part was rebuilt in brick and returned to use (see above) in the mid-1950s. In more recent years, the mill complex was further expanded to the right and adapted to grind animal feed. And then, a few years ago when the mill closed and conversion for residential use was being considered, another disastrous fire destroyed the eighteenth-century timber-framed section that had survived the 1951 conflagration. The modern picture shows the gutted site with hoardings erected around it for safety. A decision is still to be made on the future of the rest of the building.

Thanington Water Pumping Station. This building could be found between the Canterbury suburb of Wincheap and the once outlying village of Thanington. It was originally built in 1869 to a design first employed for the construction of Crimean War forts. The first picture, from the late nineteenth century, shows the frontage of the original building. Note the tall chimney, in an age when the pumping activities were undertaken by steam engine. In 1924, the pumping station was extended and soon boasted four bore holes that, at their peak, supplied around 40 per cent of the water supply for Canterbury, Whitstable and Herne Bay. And then in 1994, the establishment of a park-and-ride site opposite meant the pumping station's main entrance had to be changed. This necessitated the demolition of the building's settling tanks, so that access to the rear could be established. The lower photograph was taken after the partial demolition (left), in February 1996.

In 1997, it became necessary to conduct emergency repairs on the four subterranean bore holes and the water company applied for permission to demolish the rest of the building to facilitate this. Despite local protests, demolition was granted, as the local supply was thought to be under threat. The above view dramatically illustrates the start of this work. Note the remains of former ornamental ponds in the foreground. One of the council's conditions, on allowing demolition, was that a facsimile replacement building be constructed on the site following repair work. This was eventually honoured and the new structure is now a furniture warehouse, as can be seen below. The new building also incorporates the pumping station's original 1869 date stone.

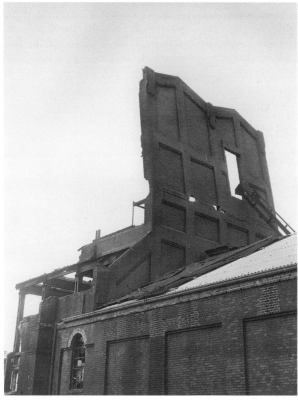

The Gasworks. The premises of the Canterbury Gas and Water Company once occupied a large area on either side of Castle Street. However, the main coal gas producing plant was situated to the rear of the site, on the corner of Gas Street and Church Lane St Mildred's. It is featured here in a 1950s drawing by Chris Law from the junction of Church Lane with Wincheap Grove. This lofty edifice was of relatively recent construction, probably having been built in the 1930s, and could be seen for miles around from the south-west approaches to the city. However, by August 1960, this part of the gasworks had become redundant and was demolished, on the left, taken from Gas Street.

Following demolition of the main gas plant, the remaining office buildings of the company, which fronted on to Castle Street, were retained for a few years more. They are seen here in 1968, before the final closure and clearance of the site. At this time, other gasworks buildings, as well as a sizeable gasometer, could still be found on the opposite site of the street (right). Following demolition, the sites of both sides of Castle Street became surface car parks. And then, in the late 1970s, a low-rise multi-storey car park, screened by new terraced houses, was constructed on the main gasworks site. This clever development can be seen in the current view. To this day, the gasometer site opposite is still a surface car park.

The Star Brewery. Above are two late 1920s views of the Star Brewery complex of G. Beer & Rigden Ltd, which stood between the city wall and the top end of Broad Street. This was a time when, according to one former brewery employee, the water in Canterbury had become unsuitable for brewing. Consequently, the brewery was closed in 1930 and its massive fortress-like premises demolished. This freed the site for the city's first official car park, but also allowed for the widening of Broad Street, as the initial stage in an attempt to construct a pre-war ring road. The modern view below shows that since the Broad Street car park was established in the early 1930s, little has changed.

Dane John Brewery. This
sturdy Victorian brewery
once occupied a city-centre
site, on the large plot
between Watling Street and
Marlowe Avenue. Its
imposing corner façade,
c. 1900, is shown in the
top picture. The brewery
lasted a bit longer than its
Broad Street rival and
closed in 1936, after which
Mackeson's transferred its
operations to Hythe.
Demolition followed and
the City Council bought the
site, declaring its interest in
building council houses
there. Yet by 1945, this
plan had changed, for the
City Council its intention
started of rehousing itself in
an impressive new Civic
Centre. But local
government reorganisation
in the early 1970s put paid
to such grandiose desires.
For the rest of the twentieth
century, the site became a
surface car park, and it was
still possible to see remains
of the former brewery
building in the site's
perimeter wall, as shown in
the middle photograph.
A replacement United
Reformed Church finally
appeared here in the last
few years (see Chapter 7).

The Lime Kiln Works. This quarry was situated on the edge of the city's Wincheap suburb, at the end of the appropriately named Lime Kiln Road. The lime works were operated by Frank Cooper Ltd, which also had offices in Watling Street. Note the processing shed at the top left, with the two main kilns just visible on the far right. The lime works closed in the early 1960s and most of the buildings were demolished in September 1965. The kilns were found to be baked solid and it took great effort to bring them down. In recent years, the former quarry has been subject to landfill, although a few years ago it was still possible to find remains of former lime works buildings, as shown below.

The Friars Fellmongers. This largely timber-constructed building was the premises of Green & Co., fellmongers, and was situated off Friar's Bridge on a site that had once been the Blackfriars churchyard (see Chapter 1). The slatted wooden sides had been specially designed to allow air circulation for the drying of woollen fleeces. Sadly, in 1940, the family firm was forced to close after its premises had been taken over by the wartime Wool Marketing Board. Oddly, the building was subsequently pressed into use as a timber store, but this new use did much to hasten the building's destruction by incendiary bombs in the June 1942 Blitz. Below is the Friends' Meeting House, which occupies the riverside site today.

Wincheap BRS Depot. In the old picture of May 1961, the large three-storey Georgian house to the left was in use as the offices of British Road Services. It stood at a point where Castle Street segued into Wincheap Street. At the beginning of the twentieth century, it had been a dwelling known as The Cedars. The house was then taken over by local hauliers C. & G. Yeoman. Later, on nationalisation of all road haulage businesses in 1949, the premises were subsumed by BRS. Sadly, the former Cedars and the row of terraced houses to its right were demolished in the early 1960s to make room for the new ring road – the Rheims Way – and its approaches to the new Wincheap Roundabout. The modern picture was taken on a Sunday, when traffic was flowing more smoothly than it usually does at this busy location.